Creative
Paper Projects

Creative
Paper Projects

Sandi Reinke

of

loose ends L.L.C.

Sterling Publishing Co., Inc. New York

A Sterling/Chapelle Book

Chapelle, Ltd.:
  Jo Packham
  Sara Toliver
  Cindy Stoeckl

Editors: Karla Haberstich, Kelly Ashkettle

Art Director: Karla Haberstich

Graphic Illustrator: Kim Taylor

Copy Editors: Anne Bruns, Marilyn Goff

Photography: Diane Dietrich-Leis, Dietrich Photography

Staff: Areta Bingham, Donna Chambers, Emily Frandsen, Lana Hall, Susan Jorgensen, Jennifer Luman, Melissa Maynard, Barbara Milburn, Lecia Monsen, Suzy Skadburg, Kim Taylor, Linda Venditti, Desirée Wybrow

Library of Congress Cataloging-in-Publication Data

Reinke, Sandi
Creative paper projects / Sandi Reinke.
    p. cm.
"Sterling/Chapelle Book."
Includes Index.
ISBN 1-4027-1032-1
1. Paper work. 2. Interior decoration. 3. House furnishings. I. Title.
TT870.R44 2004
745.54--dc22

                    2004005350

10 9 8 7 6 5 4 3 2 1
Published by Sterling Publishing Co., Inc.
387 Park Avenue South, New York, NY 10016
©2004 by Sandi Reinke
Distributed in Canada by Sterling Publishing
c/o Canadian Manda Group, One Atlantic Avenue, Suite 105
Toronto, Ontario, Canada M6K 3E7
Distributed in Great Britain by Chrysalis Books Group PLC,
The Chrysalis Building, Bramley Road, London W10 6SP, England
Distributed in Australia by Capricorn Link (Australia) Pty. Ltd.
P. O. Box 704, Windsor, NSW 2756, Australia
Printed and Bound in China
All Rights Reserved

Sterling ISBN 1-4027-1032-1

If you have any questions or comments, please contact:
Chapelle, Ltd., Inc.,
P.O. Box 9252, Ogden, UT 84409
(801) 621-2777 • (801) 621-2788 Fax
e-mail: chapelle@chapelleltd.com
web site: www.chapelleltd.com

loose ends®
2065 Madrona Ave. SE
Salem, OR 97302
web site: www.looseends.com

FOREWORD

Sandi Reinke is one of a kind. She has the face of an angel, a hairdo that looks as if she'd been struck by lightening on the way down, and an imagination that won't quit. I'm so glad that she finally decided to write this book.

Sandi and I first met back in January of 1995 at HIA, the craft industry's big trade show. My television show on the new HGTV network had only been on the air a short time, so Sandi didn't know who I was and I knew nothing about her or **loose ends.** However, when I saw their booth at the show, I immediately became lost in it. It was packed full of so many interesting and unusual looking "things." I found each item I saw more intriguing than the one before, even if I didn't know what it was. It took me a while to realize that almost everything I was looking at had something to do with paper. It was either covered with paper or made with paper, or it was just beautiful and unusual paper. That was the beginning of a long and happy relationship that joined Sandi's world of paper with my world of television

Over the years, Sandi has become not only a good friend but the perfect television guest. The producers love her. We always know she will have some interesting and unusual project. It may be goofy, but it will be fascinating. It may sound strange, yet turn out to be something not only wonderfully unique but practical as well. It may be just the thing to turn on the imagination and think of other things you might never have thought of before. That's what Sandi does. She stimulates the imagination—and then shows you how to follow through.

That, too, is what Sandi's book is all about— stimulating the imagination and trying new things. Cover a rock with handmade paper? Well, why not? Or a sugar bowl with paper that looks like a giraffe? Or how about a retro looking clock and lamp base and table scarf, all made with paper? Or a paper pillow? Ever tried one of those before? If you get to wondering about what kind of paper can possibly be strong enough to do the job and still be pretty enough to make you want it, there are stories about that as well.

I suddenly realized: Sandi's book is not only filled with fun and funny and fabulous projects but there are paragraphs and pages filled with fascinating information as well. Here is a craft book that is also a good read!

Enjoy!
Carol Duvall

TABLE OF CONTENTS

The Beginnings

THOUGHTS ABOUT PAPER & LIFE
(how to use this book and other bits of useful information)

I originally fell totally in love with paper one rainy afternoon in 1990, when Art, my husband, and I were in Taiwan working on getting our fledgling import business started. We had met and were working with a wonderful young Chinese man who was also just getting started in his own export business—instant kismet for the three of us. On a whim, he took us to a showroom of a friend of his, who made wonderful papers in the mountains of Taiwan exclusively for the Japanese market. Actually, we were only going to the showroom to escape the torrential rains and to have afternoon tea with friends, but one look at the beautiful papers stacked everywhere and we were hooked. In Japan there is the delightful custom of taking great care with the wrapping and presentation of the gift, oftentimes it being more important than the gift itself. Everywhere we looked we saw wonderful applications of this sensitivity to the individual characteristics and personalities of the different papers. So enchanted were we that we made the two-day arduous trip into the Taiwanese mountains to see the papers being made, handcrafted in the same way they had been for centuries.

It took almost a year to convince this master papermaker that yes, we Americans also appreciated his special papers, and at last he agreed to do business with us. That was the beginning and like most addictions, it just got stronger. We continued on from there, looking for and adding wonderful papers from other countries as we found them. It has always been our custom to know and work with our papermakers, frequently working out new designs, colors, and textures with them. As Art and I travel to remote parts of the planet, this is always one of the most favorite aspects of our work. It is a joy and privilege to know and work with artisans that are not only preserving many of the early papermaking techniques, but also developing wonderful new ideas as they add their own creativity to this ancient craft.

Today **loose ends** carries over 800 different handmade papers and we are adding to this all the time. In addition to our extensive collection of handmade papers, we also produce our own exclusive line of paper called Project Paper. Designed and developed by us specifically for use in paper-craft applications, Project Paper has some very unique properties. Our designs are developed to create specific effects when they are distressed and applied to other surfaces. The paper is printed here in Oregon on a recycled kraft with water-soluble inks and it has the advantage of being available in a variety of configurations, from 20" x 30" sheets to bulk rolls 30" wide and 417' long. Because it is a machine-made product, it is also very economical to work with.

ABOVE: Our Paper Room is filled with Handmade Papers, Project Papers, Abaca, organic fibers, ribbons, twines and assorted googahs and embellishments.

We endeavor to always be pushing the envelope on what you can do with paper. It is so versatile and relatively inexpensive, and some absolutely incredible effects can be achieved even by a beginner. If there is any one rule, it is to not be afraid—it is, after all, only paper; and most "mistakes" can either be corrected, redone, or in many cases, actually preferred! We hope this book inspires you to look at paper in a new way and to look at the everyday objects around you with new eyes for the possibilities that lie in wait.

To make your journey through this book easier, we are beginning with a bit of info about the different papers, using found images, and then our General Techniques & "loose Lingo." This will give you our basic techniques so we don't have to be long-winded and redundant in many of the instructions. We also define a few "loose terms," words that have a specific meaning to us, and soon to you, as you meander through the projects and ideas ahead. **loose ends** designs and produces many different things and we used many of our specific items such as papers and trims. You will often find these product names in the materials list, but you should not be afraid to work with other brands to create your own look. We may have used a tin petrol can, but you could use an old metal teapot or a new plastic pitcher. Let our ideas be your starting point for looking with a new eye at all that stuff you've been saving. You will also find, interspersed throughout the book, occasional errant observations recorded in our Reality Reminders, and last-minute thoughts will be tucked into our design tips. These are just little extras that we have found along the way that didn't seem to fit anywhere else.

design tip:
· We are big believers in keeping our arts-and-crafts supplies where they are accessible and convenient to use and also visually stimulating.

We hope this book will stimulate and fuel your own imagination. We don't really expect that many folks will actually want to sleep in our moss- and paper-covered bed, but let the ideas here be jumping off points for fun, creative, and yes, even useful things that you can do with paper, maybe in ways that had never occurred to you before. We have a definitive statement here at **loose ends**: "Imagination is more important than information," and believe me, that is a credo that we live by.

Because we have a predisposition to fantasy and flights of imagination, as this book began to evolve in our heads, we were unable to keep the projects in a tidy order. One idea suggested another, then story lines came to us, and before we knew it we would have a full-blown little world, complete with its own cast of characters. We have chosen to present the projects in this way, hoping that as you read them, they will delight and entertain as much as "inform and instruct," perhaps suggesting ideas to you for your own life story. Happy creating!

ABOVE: Old Mexican cupboards in our **loose ends** studio hold paints, glues, and other goodies. Walls get covered in projects, sketches, found objects, etc., providing endless mental fodder.

HANDMADE PAPER

You can divide people into two groups—those who are crazy about handmade paper and those who are not; and I strongly suspect that the latter simply haven't been exposed to this most seductive of mediums.

loose ends currently produces and stocks over 800 different handmade papers. We include in this category papers that are partially produced on machinery that is so ancient that no one knows how some of it was originally made. There are hand-painted papers and papers that have wax added to provide a partial transparency. There are papers with bits of bamboo, exotic foliage, full leaves, or colorful blossoms. There are papers with textures that are created by raindrops on wet pulp, and papers that look like quilted fabric. Some papers are so gossamer thin that they are just "whispers" of color, while others have heavy bark and other fibers laminated to them, producing a paper that is almost more like a building material. The one thing that they all have in common, though, is their ability to seduce and enchant. Once hooked on handmade papers, you will find that they are a bit like potato chips: no one is happy with just a few!

loose ends produces most of its handmade papers in the Far East. It is a very labor-intensive activity and although there are papermakers here in the States, the "handmade" nature of the product limits the production capacity of most individual artists.

Art and I travel to a number of Asian countries to work with the best papermakers we can find. One of the most wonderful aspects of working with producing handmade paper is the opportunity we personally have to interact and participate in these very different cultures. On one of our trips to a local papermaker's factory, we were able to help our maker's grandfather beat the coconut pulp with wooden mallets, then watch as our papers were being "pulled," "couched" and then put on the family's clothesline to dry along with the father's underwear!

Many of our paper collections are the end product of an entire village or community of people. Each maker (or village) will usually have a specialty or "signature" type of paper that they produce, so consequently we usually find ourselves working with over 20 different makers at any given time. We know our makers personally and work with them, often in remote areas, to bring our ideas and their creativity together. I sometimes think that I must have been very, very good in a past life to get to do this "work"!

loose ends HANDMADE PAPER GUARANTEE
Handmade paper whether ours or someone else's is from organic and natural materials. Since the nature of this product is subject to the weather, season, and other whims of Mother Nature, we can guarantee that it will probably NOT be consistent in color or texture from one piece or one batch to the next.

REMINDER:
Handmade paper brings a whole new meaning to the term "dye lot."

PROJECT PAPER

Years ago, I became absolutely obsessed with wanting to create some frames that looked like they had been fashioned out of exotic animal skins. However, the real thing was totally out of the question for ethical reasons, to say nothing of the economic ones, so I looked in vain for any type of paper patterns that would work.

Well, you know what they say: "If you want something done right, do it yourself." So we did. We knew the look we were going after was not "one dimensional;" we needed texture, but we were working with a printed paper. So we designed our patterns to look as much as possible like the real thing, even when they were still smooth and flat, but to really come into their own when they were distressed. We worked with soft subdued colors in water-soluble inks; and instead of printing on standard bleached paper, we chose natural kraft for our "canvas." The results were very realistic-looking designs that were also ecologically responsible.

One thing led to another and soon the Wild Things collection had cheetahs, tigers, and snow leopards romping with zebras and giraffes. If we could do it with fauna, then why not flora? Soon the Rough Stuff collection followed, with patterns resembling birch bark and bougainvillea blossoms. By now, we were on a roll, and today we have Project Paper that resembles old leather, the patina of weathered Tuscan walls, and the early nineteenth-century exotic romance of French postcard art.

We have called for Project Papers in the materials lists throughout this book. You may substitute similar papers, but they may not distress in the same way.

One last word about Project Paper: Once it has been distressed it really seems to be tough and long-lasting. We distressed a long swath of Cheetah Wild Things for our Far Out of Africa bed. The photo shoot took place in early May. We never got around to taking the swath of Cheetah down and it stayed up all summer and into the late fall. It dealt with blistering hot sun, rain, high winds and two wild hail storms. The photos show how it still looked in early October!

Now think of all the things YOU could do with Project Paper.

BELOW & RIGHT: These photos were taken after the Project Paper had been out in the garden for six months. As you can see, many little slits developed along all the "distress" wrinkles. This piece also went through two fairly vigorous hailstorms and the "cuts" may have been caused by the hailstones.

VINTAGE VISIONS & VIEWS

My sister and I had the incredibly good luck to be born to parents who were collectors—collectors of everything. My mom collected antique dolls, beaded bags from the '20s, and vintage children's books. She also just as avidly (sometimes more so) collected driftwood from the beaches we walked and bits of moss, leaves and twigs from forest forays. My love and appreciation for organic material was imprinted in my genes.

Dad was a collector of stamps, books, old glass and china, and what is known as antique "paper ephemera." Everyone has childhood memories of how they think of their parents. My mental image of my father is seeing him working in his "bookroom," with thousands (yes, thousands) of books filling the bookshelves and the floor literally covered with piles of the overflow, small trails meandering through the stacks. Dad would usually be standing at the table he worked on, tweezers in hand and large stamp albums spread out in front of him. I would wander in to ask a question and he would stop what he was doing, tweezers midair, and look up at me over the top of his glasses. This is one of the strongest and most cherished images I carry of him. Since he had collected stamps since he was 12 years old, my mother, sisters and I were all quite worried about what he would do with himself when he suddenly decided 40+ years later to sell his collections. Not to worry; he moved on to antique postcards without ever missing a beat. It is from his years of accumulating those images that appealed to him that we have put together our very special Vintage Visions & Views Collection.

ABOVE: Here's an example of projects made with Vintage Visions & Views. We used our "Tricycle Tommy" image both for the Memory Journal and Memory Boxes, and just enlarged or reduced it to fit. The Journey Journal is a Saddlestitch album backed with a piece of Banyon Bark Project Paper and embellished with our "Leaving Duluth" image. All the text for these projects was printed out from a computer, then photocopied onto pieces of handmade paper and torn out. Everything was adhered with premixed water-based wallpaper paste. Detailed instructions are the same as for the Chorus Girl Wall Art project on page 65.

GENERAL TECHNIQUES & "loose LINGO"

There are certain techniques that we use over and again, and although the finished project and effect will vary greatly, the underlying techniques will not. Following are our basics including a bit of "loose lingo"—words we use that have a meaning specific to working with our papers. As you read various project instructions you may want to refer back to this section to refresh your memory. So let's get going. . . .

VINTAGE IMAGES

We have used these in many of our projects, but you may find wonderful old postcards or photographs in your own family albums. Rather than letting them gather dust or slowly turn yellow from neglect, give them a new life. Use your own history to make a "treasures" box, turn a wonderful image that you treasure into a floor cloth or decorate a flea-market find with a special "vision."

HANDMADE PROJECT PAPERS

As you work with handmade paper, you will find that there are big differences in how any individual paper responds to various treatments. Some of those that look so fragile and thin that you are almost afraid to touch them, turn out to be tough little characters; and others that look like they should take anything will turn into oatmeal in your hands the instant they get wet. We always advise people to experiment with the paper they want to work with before they get too far into a project. Papers with long fibers will stand up to lots of handling and moisture. Short-fibered papers will "mush" relatively fast, but can still be used as long as you know beforehand how they will react.

Since paper pulp can be made from almost any fiber, the diversity is endless; and even with the same fibers, there will be variances from one batch to the next and certainly from one season to the next as the organic material itself changes. This is the beauty, romance, and mystique of handmade paper and it has prompted us to offer the following observation and guarantee.

WHAT CAN YOU DO WITH PROJECT PAPER?

. . . Project Paper is printed on a medium-weight natural kraft that is ideal for any type of giftwrap application.

. . . If you are a scrapbooker, Project Paper is great for adding visual texture and pattern to your pages.

. . . We have used Project Paper instead of wallpaper to create unique surfaces. (Be sure to use a wallpaper liner first.)

. . . An interior designer sent us photos of a "zebra" kitchen floor she created with Project Paper.

. . . Use an iron-on interfacing and sew with Project Paper.

. . . Distress Project Paper and the sky's the limit. (We have been known to remark, "If it doesn't move on its own, we will cover it with paper!")

DISTRESSING

You will see this term used repeatedly throughout the book. It is one of our original methodologies. We use it in varying degrees on many different types of papers and to achieve a wide variety of effects. It is basically nothing more than wrinkling, wadding and crumpling the paper or image you are working with. Every paper will take to this treatment somewhat differently, however; and when working with a paper you are unfamiliar with, it is important to begin slowly and gently, working up to more strongly distressed states.

Our Project Papers were designed with distressing in mind to bring out their full design potential. They can take a tremendous amount of wrinkling and crumpling. We recommend spritzing Project Paper first with a misting bottle and water. If we are working with long pieces (and we often distress 20'–30' pieces of Project Paper), we will spritz both sides of the paper first, letting the moisture soften the paper. We distress them by twisting them tightly all the way to the end, then shaking out the twists. If more distressing is desired, we retwist the length of paper the other way.

Handmade papers will vary greatly in the degree of distressing that they can handle. Although twisting works very well on Project Paper, we do not recommend it for handmades. Begin distressing any handmade paper by wadding, then opening, then wadding again. If the paper is a bit stiff, you can spritz it lightly to help soften the fibers.

We also frequently distress our Vintage Visions or other images. Again, you want to wad these up very gently at first, then open and continue wadding and opening until the desired degree of distressing is reached.

In general, distressing will soften your paper, yet paradoxically, it will often make it stronger and more pliable. Distressed papers, either Project Paper or many handmade papers, can actually be used in sewing applications and they usually work better after they have been distressed. If you are going to apply any of these papers to walls or large surfaces, the distressing removes the very frustrating problem of getting all the wrinkles out, because the wrinkles are part of the design.

After distressing any of the above mediums, you can add paints or washes to antique the surface, drip metallics down the surface to catch in the wrinkles, or simply use the textured surface as part of your design. As you work with the various papers, you will discover many uses for this technique.

LEFT: Our Zebra Rug from our Far Out of Africa project on page 24.

17

GLUING & ADHESIVES

The best type of adhesive for a project depends on the paper you are using, the effect you are going for, and, of course, the use the project will have after completion. Below are the main adhesives we have used for the projects in this book.

ABOVE: The porcelain-like finish on this lamp base was created by tearing bits of handmade paper and then sealing them with liquid laminate.

ADHESIVE #1: "GLUTER" (GLUE & WATER)

Gluter is my shortened name for "water-soluble white glue and water mixture" (glue + water). To make it, mix about 70% of any water-soluble white glue and 30% water. A pea-soup consistency is usually just about right.

My favorite way to work with gluter is to dip the paper pieces directly into it, gently squeeze out the excess and apply the paper to a surface. The other most common way is to brush the gluter onto the back of the paper with either a bristle or sponge brush, apply the paper to the surface and then apply another coat of gluter on top.

You will often get very different effects from these two techniques. Dipping the paper may dramatically change the color of some handmade papers, and if they have very short fibers, it may turn them to oatmeal. This is not always a bad thing, because it will let you mold the paper onto a surface for an entirely different effect. Test a bit of the papers before using them to experiment with their characteristics.

ADHESIVE #2: WALLPAPER PASTE

Premixed water-based wallpaper paste is less sticky than gluter, but stays damp long enough to allow you to keep reworking a piece. This makes it ideal for working with a large area, like a hallway. To some extent, it can be used interchangeably with gluter, but it can be too heavy for some papers and have a tendency to tear them. It's also more expensive, so it is best saved for big projects where the savings of time and effort are worth the expense.

ADHESIVE #3: LIQUID LAMINATE

Liquid laminate will dry to a hard satin finish that will make the paper seem almost like part of the surface that it is covering. A few finishing coats over a project like a lamp base will make the paper look almost like china or porcelain.

Liquid laminate is especially nice to use on metal and glass projects, but does not adhere well to wood. Although it is more expensive, a little bit goes a long way, and it gives a translucent quality to the paper that you do not get with the other techniques.

FINISHES

The finish you use for your project will depend on how you plan to use it and the final appearance you want it to have. If it is decorative and will only get mild use, a finish may not be needed. If it is made with gluter, the surface may feel slightly sticky, so if it will be handled, it is best to use an acrylic sealer, which is available with a matte, satin or high-gloss finish. Wallpaper-paste projects usually don't need a sealer, except for decorative purposes. If either gluter or wallpaper-paste projects will be in a damp area, however, it is best to seal them. Liquid laminate is almost its own finish and sealant, so projects made with this adhesive will not need a sealer unless you want a high-gloss finish.

Most craft stores carry acrylic sealers in small sizes, and these are very convenient to use; but for bigger projects, you may want to get a larger container at a home improvement store. Think about what it is that you want to do, then go shopping and see what all your alternatives are.

DECKLE

Deckle is a jagged uneven edge that is the hallmark of handmade papers. The edge is created when the wet pulp is dried on a screen. The pulp flows out to the edges of the screen's frame, but it is never evenly distributed with knife-sharp edges, and so all hand-thrown papers will have this ragged edge.

When you cut pieces of your handmade paper for use in projects, you can re-create the deckle appearance by tearing rather than cutting the paper. We often recommend throughout our instructions that you tear off all straight edges. When covering an item with paper you will find that the torn edges seem to meld into each other, without any place where you can see one paper stopping and another one starting. By doing this before you begin, you won't have to try to get rid of straight edges when your hands are full of glue.

For many projects, just tearing the paper into bits and pieces is fine. However, you will find there are times when you want specific geometric shapes that better lend themselves to cutting, but you do not want the cut edge. A very simple way to solve this is to fold the paper forward and backward to make a sharp edge, and then dampen it on both sides with a cotton swab, paintbrush or a finger. Give it a moment for the moisture to soak in, then open and flatten the paper. With the palms of both hands on either side of the damp fold line, GENTLY pull the two parts of the paper away from each other. If the paper has material in or on it that won't easily tear (long tough plant fibers, silk threads, or even waxed designs on the surface), you can weaken these spots with a craft knife or the tip of a pair of scissors to help them tear along the line. This will let you create edges that very closely resemble the original deckle edge and keep the ambience of the handmade paper.

ABOVE: The edges of Fish Project Paper were deckled so they would blend into each other when adhered to this napkin weight.

CHAPTER ONE

FAR OUT OF AFRICA

The journey had been long, dusty and difficult. When the rains came, she feared she might never be dry again. But finally they arrived at their destination, a lovely old plantation house surrounded by exotic flora and fauna. Cool breezes were allowed to waft through the rooms, bringing the lightly perfumed air into the farthest reaches of the house. But her favorite place was her own bedroom. This she shared with no one. It was her own private escape, where she could lounge on her moss bed and zebra coverlet, sipping jasmine tea from a leopard mug, and nibbling on—what else?—animal cookies. Here she could read Kipling while she gazed out across the savanna, occasionally getting a glimpse of the rare "zebra goose" jealously watching over her nest of tiger-print eggs. And here, too, she might catch sight of the mysterious stranger who sometimes appeared, always wearing his signature zebra vest. Who could he be? She feared knowing, yet feared even more that she might never know.

RIGHT: Animal patterns have been livening up interiors and adding a touch of the exotic ever since that first caveman (or woman) added a few stripes to provide visual interest to the cave wall. Wild Things Project Paper is as close as you can get to the real thing without the roar! Dampen and distress these and you will have to touch them to remember they're paper!

✂ design tip:

- The trick to working with and getting the best effects from the Wild Things Project Paper is to "distress, distress, distress"! The more you work these particular patterns, the more realistic they become.

The ultimate fantasy bedroom, this one has loads of ideas for the adventurer in you! Virtually all of the projects, including our "pelt," have been made with paper or tissue. And, although it is paper, with a bit of care, even the vest and goose should last for years. We chose to create a fabulous safari bedroom, but any of these ideas could be used equally effectively in other rooms of the house. The "pelt" makes a great faux substitute for the real thing on a wall in a man's office or den. The bed tray could just as easily sit on a desk or even on a kitchen counter. And a frame would be a great place to gather up all those photos of last year's vacation, especially if it happened to have been in Africa (or Adventureland at Disney World!).

Animal prints are now considered almost a neutral and can easily accompany and complement almost any decor, from elegant to rustic, so let your imagination go and see what WILD ideas you can come up with.

Reality Reminder:

God is not really an artist. He invented the giraffe, the elephant, the cat. He has no real style. He just keeps trying things.

—Pablo Picasso

What? The moss bedspread? Well, that is a wonderful product called Moss Cloth. It is simply sphagnum moss that has been adhered to a sticky mesh background that holds the moss in place. You could easily make your own by painting a layer of white glue on a fabric backing, spreading a fairly thick layer of moss and allowing it to dry. (P.S. Whether you make it yourself or buy the premade Moss Cloth, this will FOREVER be a somewhat messy item as the moss will always be flaking off.)

WILD THINGS PAPER PILLOWS

We used a number of simple pillow patterns to make these decorative throw pillows. The Wild Things Project Paper will become quite soft as you distress it. Although the following directions are for the Giraffe Pillow, any combination of animal-print patterns would be equally effective.

✂ design tips:

· All types of small pods or even stones look great as accents on these pillows.

· Rough burlap looks particularly good with the Wild Things patterns. Try combining these two materials in other ways (throws, etc.).

MATERIALS

. 1 yard iron-on interfacing

. 2 sheets Giraffe Project Paper

. glue gun and glue sticks

. iron

. pillow insert or stuffing

. pods or stones for accents

. scissors

. sewing machine

. simple pillow pattern

. trim

. Velcro closures

INSTRUCTIONS

GIRAFFE PILLOW

1. Distress the paper, allowing it to dry before continuing.

2. Smooth out the dry distressed paper with your hands, working it out with your fingers to be as flat as possible. Iron the interfacing onto the wrong side of the paper.

3. Cut out pillow pattern from the paper and sew wrong sides together as if working with cloth.

4. Trim corners and curves and wrinkle the area with your hand to soften it, then carefully turn the paper to the right side.

5. If your pattern has an opening, hot-glue on a Velcro closing.

6. Stuff your pillow with the insert.

7. Attach accents and trim to mock a button closure and fabric trim.

8. With a minimum amount of care, your paper pillows should be able to last for years.

VARIATIONS

. We used an envelope pillow pattern and Zebra Project Paper for this pillow, and Cheetah Project Paper for the flap lining, adding some chocolate pods for decoration.

. Cheetah Project Paper was used for this small rectangular pillow pattern. The center closure is tied off with a few strands of cinnamon abaca twine.

. The bolster pillow was created by distressing Snow Leopard Project Paper, tearing the sides, gently rolling it around a cotton form (jelly-roll style), hot-gluing the end "seam," and tying off the sides with a hank of natural raffia.

. Our last variation combines Tiger Project Paper and burlap cloth. We cut two pieces of the burlap 24" x 18" and a piece of paper the same size. We then fringed the sides of the burlap and distressed and slightly tore the sides of the paper. Using fusible webbing to attach the paper (right side up) to the top of one of the burlap pieces, we then sewed the two burlap squares together, leaving an opening for stuffing. We stuffed the pillow and hand-stitched the opening closed.

ZEBRA RUG

See photograph on page 25.

This one requires a bit of imagination before you begin. There really is no pattern for a zebra pelt, so we simply drew a very rough sketch of the shape. The main thing to remember is to have curves and definitions where the legs and tail would be. Don't worry if your drawing skills aren't what you think they should be; the pattern alone will carry the idea, and this is such a fun piece that can be used anyplace where it won't get heavy foot traffic. We have played with these under tables, on walls and, of course, as a fabulous bed throw!

MATERIALS

. 2½ yards cotton batting

. 6 yards fusible webbing

. 20' burlap cloth

. 20' roll Zebra Project Paper

. iron

. scissors

. sewing machine

Reality Reminder:
I wouldn't have lived my life the way I did if I was going to worry about what people were going to say.

—Ingrid Bergman

INSTRUCTIONS

1. Distress the paper. Let dry.

2. Cut three lengths of the paper, each 90" long.

3. Sew the three together, side by side lengthwise, making a 90" square.

4. Iron one side of the fusible webbing onto the back side of the paper, then iron the other side of the fusible webbing onto the cotton batting.

5. Tear this large square into a pelt shape with four legs, a tail, and part of a neck.

6. Iron another piece of the fusible webbing onto the exposed side of the cotton batting and set aside.

7. Sew the two pieces of burlap cloth together lengthwise, then iron them to the cotton batting on the pelt.

8. Cut the burlap cloth to the same basic shape as your paper pelt, leaving about 3" of the cloth beyond the edges of the pelt, and fray the edges to create a fringed finish.

ZEBRA BED TRAY

We LOVE old cupboard doors! There are so many things you can make out of them. If you don't have an old one around, check out lumber supply houses that frequently have "seconds" that can be picked up for a song (and they're usually pretty inexpensive too, in case you don't sing).

MATERIALS

. 1 sheet Zebra Project Paper

. 2 simple brass door handles

. 4 brass doorstops

. black permanent marker

. cabinet door with raised trim

. drill and small bit

. gluter

. scissors

. screws

INSTRUCTIONS

1. Distress the paper and hand-press flat.

2. Cut to fit on the flat area inside trim on door.

3. Dip the paper in the gluter and glue down on the door. Wrinkles in the paper are fine, but press them down with your fingers so that the surface is flat. Let dry overnight.

4. Center the door handles on either end of the door and screw in place.

5. Turn tray over and screw the doorstops into all four corners of bottom of tray.

6. Color the white rubber cap at the bottom the doorstop with the black permanent marker (black matte acrylic paint is okay too, but will chip more easily).

design tips:

• This is a great piece to simply set on a table. You can use it to accent anything from a dry floral arrangement to a tea serving setup.

• The sturdiness of the cupboard doors, handles, and doorstops makes it a good serving piece for outdoor barbecues, too!

"ON SAFARI" WALL ART

The "Africa in the '20s and '30s" look of this project was created by using vintage images. If you have old wildlife prints that you like, those would work fine in this application. Take your old prints to a copy center and have them color copied and enlarged (or reduced) to fit your board. River cane is a very lightweight relative of the more familiar bamboo; it adds a terrific handmade, almost tropical look to the finished piece. This is a great project for adding a touch of the "safari" look to a room that is not otherwise too "African."

MATERIALS

. 1 sheet Tiger Project Paper

. board, 18" x 15" (anything will work; we actually used a broken piece of old ceiling tile)

. color copies of cheetah, elephant, giraffe, ostrich, and zebra

. floral wire

. glue gun and glue sticks

. natural raffia

. picture hanger

. premixed water-based wallpaper paste

. river cane bundle

. scissors

. wide paintbrush or painting sponge

INSTRUCTIONS

1. Cut the paper approximately 2" larger than the size of the board. Distress.

2. Apply the wallpaper paste (fairly thickly) to your board. Find the middle of the paper by bringing both sides together gently, then lowering the paper onto the pasted board, center area first. Gently smooth out air bubbles with your hands as you work the paper from the middle out to the edges. Small wrinkles are no problem; just be certain to work the paper down securely to the board. Let dry.

3. Apply the wallpaper paste to the backs of the prints, and position them onto the board. The paste is fairly forgiving, and you should be able to slightly move them for the first few minutes. Smooth down and work out any air bubbles with your hands or dry painting sponge. Let dry.

4. Cut twelve pieces of river cane 23" long and six pieces 26" long.

5. Hot-glue three 26" pieces of the of river cane together, and hot-glue these bundles to the top and bottom of your board, allowing the ends to extend past the board. Do the same with the 23" pieces, allowing these ends to go over the top and bottom pieces. Trim all ends so that the lengths are slightly irregular.

6. Lash the corners together with floral wire, and anchor the corners with hot glue. Cover the wire and any glue by re-lashing with the natural raffia, knot and cut 1" ends.

7. Attach a picture hanger and hang.

✂ design tips:

• When enlarging or reducing any picture or print, remember that you can only choose one dimension (height or width), so decide which is the most critical. The other dimension will, of course, enlarge or reduce at the same percentage. This might seem obvious but I still remember the first time I gave both my desired dimensions to the clerk and he looked at me like I was slightly simple.

• And who says that your pictures always have to hang straight? The "safari style" of this project makes it a fun candidate for hanging askew!

ZEBRA GOOSE

Over the years, we have made geese, bears, bunnies, frogs, rats, pigs, and other creatures, all from standard sewing patterns, using papers instead of fabric. Most patterns will adapt to paper use quite well; just try to keep to simple lines. Project Paper works especially well, because, after it has been distressed, it becomes very flexible and malleable. Soft handmade papers are also good, but they need to be strong with long fibers. Test any paper first by lightly crumpling, twisting, etc. If it tears easily under this treatment, it probably won't hold up well when sewn. For added strength, you can also use an iron-on fusible webbing.

MATERIALS

. 1 sheet Black Project Paper

. 1 yard iron-on pellon interfacing

. 2 sheets Zebra Project Paper

. glue gun and glue sticks

. goose pattern

. pillow stuffing

. scissors

. sewing machine

design tips:

• Hems are glued down.

• To turn a piece to the right side, wrinkle it up in your hand and gently push through the opening.

• Clipping and trimming seams is very important when sewing with paper.

• Use glue gun when sewing is impossible.

• Use a stuffing tool when stuffing your animal—you are less likely to tear the paper. If you don't have a tool, use a pencil or chopstick.

INSTRUCTIONS

1. Determine the size of your pattern pieces on the papers that you will be using for your animal. Press the pellon to the uncut pieces of paper before cutting out the pattern. If necessary, cut the size of the papers down so that you will not waste the pellon.

2. Distress the papers. Let dry. Straighten and flatten with your hand. Cut a piece of the pellon to fit each of the papers and press to the back side of the papers.

3. Cut out the pattern according to the manufacturer's instructions and sew as instructed, with the following changes for working with paper, rather than cloth:

3a. If there is a long leg, neck, or arm to turn, sew one side, right sides together, then turn wrong sides together and hot-glue the other side, tucking the raw edges in as you go. Don't try to sew both sides and turn; the paper usually won't be able to take it.

3b. Simple straight lines (such as the body of the animal) can be turned, but you must clip and turn very carefully.

4. Stuff the piece with pillow stuffing and hot-glue the opening closed.

BELOW: *Zebra Goose protecting her clutch of Wild Things Spheres. Wild Things Vase in background.*

WILD THINGS SPHERES

These are silly and fun, and are a great project to do with the kids. Hang them from the ceiling, give them away as party favors, or fill a big empty pot. We have used these for everything from creating a Wild Things Christmas tree to tucking a few of them into a bowl of organic spheres, like we did for our Far Out of Africa bedroom.

MATERIALS

. 1 sheet each Wild Things Project Papers: Cheetah, Giraffe, Jaguar, Snow Leopard, Tiger, Zebra

. acrylic sealer

. balloons

. cotton string

. gluter

design tip:

• When storing spheres, it is important to put them where they will be dry, and not get crushed. Small dents can be popped back out with a pencil or my favorite tool, a chopstick! These are amazingly strong. We have some that have been recycled through many projects for at least three years.

INSTRUCTIONS

1. Distress papers and tear into small pieces, tearing off all straight edges.

2. Blow up balloons to desired sizes for the spheres, and tie a long piece of string onto each balloon.

3. Dip the paper pieces individually into the gluter and place on balloon, layering the pieces over each other until you have at least 2–3 layers of paper on the balloon. Leave a small opening at the tied end of the balloon. The more layers of paper, the stronger the sphere.

4. Let dry completely, then apply 1–2 coats of a acrylic sealer. When dry, pop the balloon and pull it out with the string.

WILD THINGS VASE

See photograph on page 30.

We have made versions of this particular vase a number of times. We have left it with the paper untouched and we have aged it by adding an acrylic wash. We have used a matte sealer for a very natural look, a satin finish when we wanted it to resemble porcelain, and a high-gloss surface when we wanted a strong contrast to the organic nature of the patterns.

MATERIALS

. 1 sheet each Wild Things Project Papers: Cheetah, Jaguar, Tiger

. acrylic paints: browns, greens, ochre

. acrylic sealer (optional)

. gluter

. papier-mâché formed vase

. small dish

. sponge

INSTRUCTIONS

1. Distress papers and tear into small workable pieces, eliminating all straight edges. Make the pieces different shapes; some long and thin, others more blocky, so that your pattern on the vase will be more interesting.

2. Dip the paper pieces individually into the gluter and apply them to the vase, varying the patterns and letting them overlap each other in a random manner.

3. Let dry overnight.

4. Take a few drops of the different shades of acrylic paint and mix together in a small dish. Add water (4–5 times as much water as paint), and lightly sponge this onto the vase to soften and blend the patterns. Let dry, then add another sponging of paint if it needs more aging.

5. If desired, you can now add a coat or two of an acrylic sealer to add a finish to the piece.

design tip:

• Anytime you are going to have to wrap your surface papers around the bottom of a piece, it is very helpful to put the item up on something that is stable enough to hold the item, but is narrower than the item's bottom. This will make it easy to wrap your paper pieces around the lower edge and tuck them under to the bottom side.

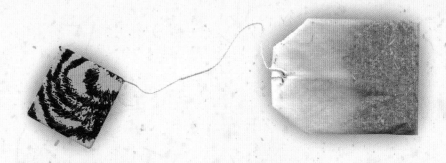

SNOW LEOPARD TEACUP & SAUCER

See photograph on page 33.

Can't you just see Meryl Streep sitting on the veranda of her African home, sipping afternoon tea and nibbling on—what else—animal cookies? We tucked the cookies into a natural-fiber, savanna cloth cache box with the same Snow Leopard Tissue Paper that we used on the cup and saucer.

These are quite usable if they are gently washed by hand (never in a dishwasher). Although we only made one for our bed tray, wouldn't a whole set of all different animal prints be cool?

MATERIALS

. 1 sheet Snow Leopard Tissue Paper

. 1 sheet Zebra Project Paper (or a
    scrap from another project)

. liquid laminate

. paintbrush

. small dish

. tea bag with label

. white cup and saucer

INSTRUCTIONS

1. Distress Snow Leopard tissue and tear into small pieces.

2. Pour a small amount of laminate into dish.

3. With a paintbrush, apply laminate to the saucer and adhere torn tissue. Paint laminate on tissue as you are layering on saucer. Cover complete top and bottom and let dry.

4. Cover the bottom of cup with the same method, working two-thirds of the way up the side of the cup, and leaving jagged torn tissue points for the edge on the cup.

5. The final touch is a zebra cover on a tea bag label. We made this by taking a very small square of the Zebra paper and gluing it to the label.

design tip:

• We used Tissue on our cup and saucer and Wild Things Project Paper on the accompanying sugar bowl. Although the patterns are the same on both papers, the finished effect is quite different. The tissues give a rather translucent and more delicate look to the finished project, which is why we like it better for the cup with its "torn pelt" points. We used paper on the sugar bowl to give it a heavier, more substantial look.

GIRAFFE SUGAR BOWL

This piece can easily stand alone or mix in nicely with a variety of other cups or mugs that you may have. Wouldn't this be fun to do on a large cookie jar?

MATERIALS

. 1 sheet Giraffe Project Paper

. liquid laminate

. paintbrush

. small dish

. sugar bowl with lid

INSTRUCTIONS

1. Distress the paper and tear into small pieces, being certain not to leave any straight edges.
2. Pour a small amount of laminate into dish.
3. Apply the paper by brushing laminate on back of paper and layering it on the lid and bowl until covered. Let dry completely.
4. Apply 2–3 more coats of laminate. Let dry.

CHAPTER TWO

FIESTA !

One of the most common questions e-mailed to us here at **loose ends** is "where do you come up with your ideas?" Mental fodder is where you find it and sometimes the smallest thing will trigger a project. Oddly enough it was actually the little flowering broom plant (at the foot of the table) in these "too hot to handle" brilliant reds, oranges, and yellows that inspired us to play with some really bold colors. An accent table seemed just the thing for these "accent" colors, and for contrast we cooled things off a bit with a sea blue jug, then heated it up again with our "Fiesta Sticks." Olé!

FIESTA CORNER TABLE

We went to a "seconds" building supply house for our kitchen cabinet door ($2.00!). The table legs can be whatever height that works for the spot where you are planning on putting the table. We added this accent table in the corner of a room that otherwise was fairly neutral in color with lots of shades of browns, creams, and taupe. Wow! What a splash of color this provided!

MATERIALS

. 2 sheets red handmade paper

. 4 unfinished wood slender table legs

. 16 large orange crinkle rose petals

. cabinet door

. drill and screws

. glue gun and glue sticks

. gluter

. paintbrush

. sandpaper

design tip:

- If you want a more "froufrou" table you can add Crinkle Rose Petals all around the edge of the table, creating a scallop trim.

INSTRUCTIONS

1. Sand the door and smooth off the rough edges.

2. Screw the legs to the underside of the door, on the four corners.

3. Tear handmade paper into workable-sized pieces.

4. Gluter can be painted onto the door first, then the paper applied; or the paper can be dipped into the gluter, then layered onto the door and legs. (This paper bleeds, so you will want to work rather quickly if you are dipping it.) Continue doing this to cover the entire table, then let dry completely.

5. After table is dry, make fancy column legs by hot-gluing four crinkle rose petals around the upper part of each leg (petals going up).

WINE JUG WITH FIESTA STICKS

Although this has a real "South of the Border" look to it, it also works surprisingly well in a French Country environment.

MATERIALS

JUG

. 1 sheet blue handmade paper

. 1 sheet yellow handmade paper

. acrylic sealer

. heavy-duty, premixed water-based wallpaper paste

. paintbrush

. sponge brush

. wine jug

FIESTA STICKS

. 2 sheets red and yellow handmade paper

. gluter

. interesting sticks

. sand or small pebbles

. sponge brush

INSTRUCTIONS

JUG

1. Tear paper into small workable pieces, leaving the yellow pieces a bit larger to make them easier to handle.

2. Sponge-brush the wallpaper paste onto the wine jug in small areas and apply layers of blue paper to the complete jug, sponge-brushing the paper as you apply it.

3. While the jug is still wet, apply pieces of the yellow paper, leaving some areas uncovered to create the desired effect. Apply more paste to gently cover the added paper.

4. Let dry overnight.

5. When dry, apply three coats of acrylic sealer, allowing the coats to dry between applications. (We used a satin finish.)

FIESTA STICKS

1. Tear the red and yellow paper into small workable pieces.

2. Sponge-brush gluter onto the sticks and squeeze the paper around all sides, working the paper into all of the interesting angles. You can dip the paper pieces into the gluter if you work very fast, but this particular paper will turn into oatmeal rather quickly and the colors will run. You will want distinct variations of orange and yellow.

3. Let dry, then arrange the sticks in your wine jug. Weigh down the wine jug by filling one third with either sand or small pebbles.

Reality Reminder:
Everyone has a photographic memory. Some just don't have film.

—Unknown

✂ design tip:

• Another fun way to use the wine jug is to hang it from an interesting cord from the ceiling, then add a few sprigs of dry hanging amaranth or some other type of cascading foliage or long grass. This is especially effective when you group three pieces together.

ABOVE: Papier-mâché forms come in all shapes and sizes. You may prefer to do a third project with a large vase shape. Just remember that papier-mâché is light and you will want to add some gravel or sand in the bottom to create stability for the tall sticks.

CHAPTER THREE

EGGCENTRIC ART

Can't really say what got us started on our "eggcentric" journey, but once we got going, there was no stopping the silly ideas that came to us. "Eggxactly what do we want to do with this?" "Only an egglomaniac would think that!" "Egglmentary my dear Watson." "What a charming and eggfective technique!" Well, you get the idea. There is just something inherently funny about eggs, and as we began to eggsplore ideas, we realized that the egg would lend itself to all kinds of egglectic and eggstravagant applications. As one eggcellent idea led to another, we became more and more eggstatic while we added eggbellishments to walls and furniture.

As we egged each other on, there just seemed to be no end to the ways we could eggcessorize our home. There were other ideas that came to us after we had finished these projects, but eggonomics stopped us from pursuing them at the time.

These are really fun to make, are great for creating a country kitchen atmosphere, and as you can see from our above ramblings, these particular projects just seem to keep suggesting other equally eggciting ideas! The bowls are handy for holding fruit, wrapped munchies, potpourri (we have one in the studio for catching those inevitable small scraps of paper), etc. The chair is really quite usable (providing you started with a sturdy specimen to begin with) since the eggs are protected by the back rungs.

Use these ideas as a starting point as you eggsplore your own imagination.

EGGCENTRIC CHAIR

First question: Can you really sit in it? Of course, as long as you make certain you have done any structural repairs that your chair might need before beginning the project. Because the eggs are nestled in between the chair rungs, they really don't get much pressure applied to them. This would also be a great corner piece if your kitchen is large enough. Leave off the cushion and you have a great tabletop or shelf for a potted plant, a stuffed chicken, or a bowl of faux eggs.

If you go shopping for a flea-market find for this project, it is a good idea to have the faux eggs you are going to use with you so that you can be certain that they will fit between the rungs of your find. We have used chicken-sized eggs, but smaller (even quail-sized) are available in most craft stores.

design tip:
• By cutting along the fringe lines on the egg-colored fabric, you can easily create ties that do not require any finishing on the edges.

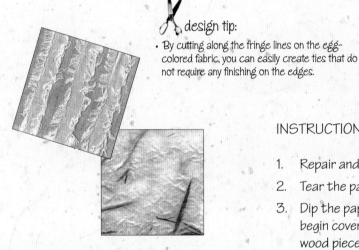

MATERIALS

. 1 yard egg-colored fabric

. 3 sheets Bamboo Project Paper

. 13 faux eggs

. glue gun and glue sticks

. gluter

. needle and thread

. pillow insert or stuffing

. scissors

. sewing machine

. simple cushion pattern

. wooden chair

INSTRUCTIONS

1. Repair and clean your chair if necessary.

2. Tear the paper into workable pieces (2"–3").

3. Dip the paper pieces individually into the gluter and begin covering chair, starting with places where the wood pieces are joined. These areas are trickiest and any awkward spots can be easily covered as you continue working on the straight planes of the chair. Let dry overnight.

4. Hot-glue the faux eggs in between the rungs. We placed them in a triangular pattern, but your chair will dictate the arrangement.

5. Cut your cushion pattern from fabric and sew together as instructed on the pattern, filling with stuffing.

6. Cut long corner ties from the egg-colored fabric by cutting along the fringe lines, leaving the edges raw.

7. Hand-stitch the ties onto the four corners.

39

CHICKEN WIRE & "CHICK" BOWL

The next time you get an invitation to a potluck and you have to bring the egg salad, we have just the bowl for you. (Of course, you will want to put a glass liner in it first.) And we guarantee NO ONE will get your offering mixed up with any of the others.

If egg salad isn't your thing, this is also a a fun container for a variety of centerpieces. Whether you fill it with potpourri, nuts and pods, faux food, or even use it as the starting point for a floral and foliage piece, it is sure to take center stage every time.

MATERIALS

. 1 sheet yellow-colored handmade paper

. 9 faux eggs

. aluminum foil

. brown paper-covered wire

. faux shell

. glue gun and glue sticks

. gluter

. light gold acrylic paint

. paintbrush

. scissors

. small bowl

. small-gauge chicken wire, 24" square

. wire cutters

INSTRUCTIONS

1. Press the chicken wire over the bowl until it takes the bowl's shape, then remove and set wire shape aside.

2. Cover outside of the bowl with aluminum foil and smooth out as much as possible.

3. Tear lime-colored paper into small workable pieces, tearing away any straight edges.

4. Dip paper into gluter and layer the bowl with the paper pieces until it is completely covered.

5. While still wet, press the chicken wire over the layer of paper on the bowl.

6. Dip more paper into gluter and apply over the chicken wire on bowl, sandwiching the wire between the two layers of paper. Press the paper into the wire so that the wire will show through in some spots. Continue doing this until the wire is covered, leaving small areas uncovered if desired. Let dry overnight.

7. Clip any sharp edges off the top of the bowl. Your edges will be uneven, adding to the charm of the piece.

8. Hot-glue eight faux eggs to the top of the bowl about 1½" apart. Leave one space for the "hatched egg."

9. The last egg will be your "hatched egg" and it has a beak and legs. To make the legs, cut two 1" pieces of paper-covered wire for the toes and two 2" pieces for the legs. Fold the 1" toe pieces in half and hot-glue the fold spot to the bottom of the 2" leg pieces.

10. Pierce small "leg" holes on either side of the bottom of egg and hot-glue the legs into the holes.

11. Paint the faux shell gold for the chick's beak. Pierce a small hole in the pointed end of the egg and hot-glue the top (round end) of the shell into the hole.

12. Glue the chick into position on top of the bowl.

design tip:

• Faux shells are one of those things that we always keep around, since they can be used for so many different things. We have put them on "beach notes" journals, used them as trim on curtains and pillows, filled glass bowls with them to anchor pillar candles, used them in an antique copper pot to hold burning incense sticks, substituted them for pebbles on the top of potted plants, framed a small shaving mirror with them. . . .

BELOW: We know that we are going to get questions about this duck—she is just something that a friend of ours sent to us from Indonesia, where he works as a geologist. Apparently this is a common art form in a number of the villages he visits. We have to admit, she seems to be the perfect companion to the Chicken Wire & "Chick" Bowl!

41

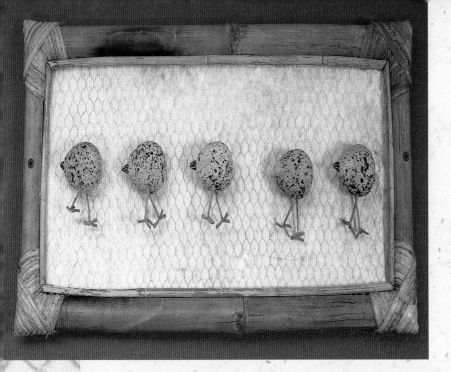

MARCHING EGGS

So what happens if you have a hen and a rooster? You usually will end up with some chicks—or at least some eggs with a chance of becoming little furry yellow friends. As a result of hanging the Hen Plaque and the Rooster Plaque in close proximity to each other, we came up with our Marching Eggs. And, of course, there is always someone who "marches to a different drummer."

MATERIALS

. 1 sheet Chicken Wire Handmade Paper

. 5 faux eggs

. 5 faux shells

. 20' brown paper-covered wire

. bamboo frame with boiserie backboard

. glue gun and glue sticks

. large needle

. paintbrush

. pencil

. scissors

. water-soluble white glue

. yellow acrylic paint

INSTRUCTIONS

1. Cut ten 1" pieces of paper-covered wire for chicken toes and ten 2" pieces for chicken legs.

2. To make the chick's feet, fold the 1" pieces in half and hot-glue the fold area to the bottom of the 2" pieces.

3. Pierce two holes in the bottom sides of each egg for the legs and hot-glue a leg in each hole.

4. Paint one faux shell yellow, leaving the others natural.

5. Push a pencil point into the pointed end of the eggs and hot-glue a shell into each egg, using the yellow shell in one of the eggs for your "one in every crowd" chick.

6. Cut an 11" x 14" piece of the paper. Remove the backboard from the frame, and using the water-soluble white glue, glue the paper to the backboard, then place into frame.

7. Hot-glue the chicks marching across the paper.

8. If you want to accent your "one in every crowd" chick, you can give him extra long legs, or maybe even a tail feather.

EGG YOLK BOWL

This bowl is similar to Chicken Wire & "Chick" Bowl on page 40, but the Illusions paper is much thinner and the chicken wire will show through as you work the paper into the wire. The variation of color in the paper really makes the finished bowl look like it was made from eggs. We used a very large stainless mixing bowl because we wanted this to be the type of container that we could fill with all kinds of other things. You can, of course, alter the size to work with whatever you have in mind.

INSTRUCTIONS

1. Press chicken wire over bowl until it takes the bowl's shape. Take wire off and set aside.

2. Cover the bowl with aluminum foil and smooth out as much as possible.

3. Tear paper into workable pieces.

4. Dip paper into gluter and begin covering bowl, placing the right side of the paper toward the bowl. (When the bowl is removed you will see the right side of the paper on the inside of your new paper bowl.) Allow the paper edges to overlap and continue until bowl is covered completely.

5. Press the chicken wire over the wet paper on the bowl.

6. Dip more paper into the gluter and press it into the wire on the bowl, right side out this time. Press paper firmly enough that the wire shows through, leaving random parts of the wire exposed at the top of the bowl. Let dry overnight.

7. Clip the edges of the wire, taking all sharp edges off. Edges will be uneven.

8. Fill up with eggs, faux or real!

MATERIALS

. 2 sheets Sunflower Illusions Handmade Paper

. aluminum foil

. gluter

. large stainless steel bowl

. small-gauge chicken wire, 36" square

. wire cutters

HEN PLAQUE

Our Hen and Rooster Plaques work together, with some of the pieces from the Hen used on the Rooster. Taken from an idea we saw in a northern Italian kitchen a few years ago, these will give a European country kitchen feel when mounted on a wall with a few faux eggs (in the Hen only please) in the tummy area.

The gloves are optional, but they really help to protect your hands when working with the sharp wire.

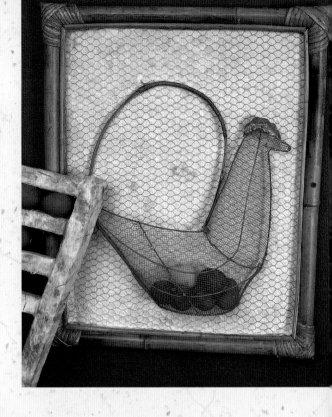

MATERIALS

. 1 sheet Chicken Wire Handmade Paper

. 1 yellow speckled faux egg

. 8 brown speckled faux eggs

. bamboo frame with boiserie backboard

. chicken-shaped basket

. curved needle

. dark gray quilting thread

. gloves

. glue gun and glue sticks

. heavy-duty craft scissors

. wire cutters

 Reality Reminder:
Remember, all small round dark objects left by the Easter Bunny are not necessarily chocolate eggs.

—Unknown

INSTRUCTIONS

1. Wearing gloves and using a wire cutter, carefully cut the chicken-shaped basket in half at the center wire from the head to the tail. Set one half aside for Rooster.

2. Trim all rough edges on the cut side of the hen.

3. Cut a piece of paper to fit frame.

4. Trim the comb on the hen's head, using scissors. Hens have a smaller comb, so make nice, neat scallops. Save the comb pieces and set aside for the rooster's waddle.

5. Tack the hen to the paper. Start at bottom of the basket, 2" from the bottom of the frame. With the curved needle and quilting thread, sew through the paper, catching the bottom wire on the hen. Pull the thread to the back side of the paper and tie off. The second tack should be at the top of the handle. The third and fourth should be on the sides, and then any place that feels loose or needs to be pulled in a bit.

6. Remove the backboard from the frame. Hot-glue the paper to the backboard, and secure back into the frame.

7. Fill the basket with eggs.

ROOSTER PLAQUE

Just like his girlfriend the Hen, our Rooster is mounted on handmade paper with real chicken wire embedded in it. Long rooster feathers and a waddle distinguish him from the fairer sex, and he NEVER expects to have to hold any faux eggs!

design tip:
• Any frame that suits your decor or design objectives will work equally well. The boiserie backboard is actually a bamboo "plywood." It has a basket-weave pattern and provides a hard solid surface to apply the chicken wire pattern paper to. If you are using a different type of frame, you will want to back the paper with something fairly stable and rigid.

MATERIALS

. ½ basket cut from hen

. 1 sheet Chicken Wire Handmade Paper

. bamboo frame with boiserie backboard

. curved needle

. dark gray quilting thread

. feathers

. instant-bonding glue

. gloves

. glue gun and glue sticks

. paintbrush

. scissors

. wire cutters

. yellow acrylic paint

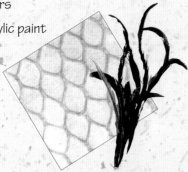

INSTRUCTIONS

1. Follow the instructions for the Hen Plaque on page 44, Steps 1–3, then tack the "rooster half" onto the chicken wire paper, following Step 5. If you are making a set, be sure the Hen and Rooster are attached so that they face each other (one facing left, one facing right).

2. Using the instant-bonding glue, glue the waddle (comb piece cut from the hen) just below the rooster's beak.

3. Remove the backboard from the frame and hot-glue the paper to the backboard, then secure back into the frame.

4. Paint one of the feathers yellow and let dry.

5. Hot-glue the feathers together, then onto the inside (back) of the rooster.

CHAPTER FOUR

WOODLAND RENDEZVOUS

It all began innocently enough. The summer concert on the edge of the woods had been lovely—an evening of light lilting Celtic music. The countryside beckoned, and the evening was so warm that late afternoon butterflies were still flitting about. The nearby gurgling creek sang on endlessly as it capered merrily over the rocks. They wandered aimlessly and shared rumors, whispering secrets of a special place—a hidden private place where moss-covered rocks nestled into lush grass. A small table and two chairs seemed to have mysteriously grown out of the very woods themselves, perhaps left by elves or wood sprites, and rumored to be there only for those with the imagination to believe. Who knew; but when they saw the tiny table, a woodland jug full of curly sticks presiding over delicate petit fours and a bottle of wine atop a moss-cloth table scarf, they knew they had found the secret place and the magic it held. They had meant only to find this place, not to linger and certainly not to sample the food and wine; but the romance enchanted them and stay they did, nibbling the sweets and sipping the wine. The warm evening air suggested how wonderful the cool creek might feel and the wine intensified the notion.

We don't know if any others, accidentally stumbling into the glen, might have been able to see this secret place, might have had the eyes and heart of a believer; but certainly anyone coming across this place that evening would surely have seen her abandoned high-heeled silver sandals, her lace stockings, and his favorite gray felt fedora.

Okay, maybe a few too many fantasy novels in my life. Our Woodland Projects are such fun, and I LOVE the excuse they give me to collect all kinds of little organic goodies. The Garden Chairs are especially fun to make; and if you have a protected area, they can last quite well outside also, adding a delightful touch to a porch, a patio or especially a garden room.

Another great thing about this particular "story line" is that it keeps you always looking at nature in new and appreciative ways. Old sticks take on new meaning, and a dried leaf or piece of bark is viewed as a possible com-plement to the strange roots you may have found last week. I find that I have become much more observant and much more in awe, even of the little things, when I am walking. Another amazing thing is that a stroll in the city can often offer almost as many possibilities as the countryside. Tree-lined streets drop all types of inter-esting pods, mushrooms spring up in the oddest places (be careful here though), and the pure wealth of diversity in leaf shapes, blossoms waiting to be pressed, etc., is mind-boggling.

You will, no doubt, find yourself thinking of other great ways to use this look. One of my favorites, that we didn't use in this book, are picture frames. They are a natural (no pun intended) for this treatment and are perfect for framing botanical or floral prints.

47

WOODLAND GARDEN CHAIRS

Finally, a place to use all those cones, pods, mosses, twigs, leaves and petals that have been hanging out for ages in a couple of discarded shoe boxes, on the top shelf of the "catch-all" closet. Our supply list has all that stuff too, in case you are one of those rare creatures who CAN go for a walk in the woods and not come back with full pockets.

MATERIALS

. 20' roll Birch Bark Project Paper

. faux dragonfly

. faux honeybees and ladybugs

. faux moss: mixed forest and green sphagnum

. faux mushrooms

. found objects: flowers, moss-covered sticks, twigs

. glue gun and glue sticks

. gluter

. old wooden chair

INSTRUCTIONS

1. The first step is to go out and find a really great old wooden chair at a yard sale or secondhand shop. Do any repairs necessary to make it safe; but don't worry about its appearance, the rougher the better.

2. Pick garden flowers, ferns, or weeds and press them to use later. Be certain to gather a variety of things, including sticks or interesting twigs.

3. Distress the paper and tear into pieces, removing all straight edges.

4. Dip the pieces individually into the gluter and cover about two-thirds of the chair, leaving places of exposed wood to add character. Allow some pieces of the paper to curl back on itself, or have thin tendrils of it "float" between the back rungs, etc. This paper will give you a very realistic base as you crumple and twist it. Let dry overnight.

5. If you have found some great-looking larger sticks, you may want to incorporate them into the structure of the chair, hot-gluing along arm areas or across the lower braces to give the piece a more organic look.

6. Hot-glue the different mosses and mushrooms to the chair as if it had grown along the chair in various areas. Cover some areas heavily, and leave other areas free, the way moss would grow.

7. Hot-glue the found objects to the chair, being certain to cluster things rather than evenly spotting them.

8. Add faux dragonfly, honeybees, and ladybugs.

WOODLAND GARDEN TABLE WITH MOSS TABLE SCARF

The trickiest part of this project is finding that perfect old crate! We were fortunate, since a friend of ours had one she had been dragging around with her since college days (we won't say how long ago that was) and she was ready for it to have a facelift. Make friends with the produce man at the corner grocery, check out fruit stands in the summer, and always remember yard sales—it's amazing what some people are willing to part with!

MATERIALS

- . 3 sheets Birch Bark Project Paper
- . 4 tassels
- . faux black lichen
- . garden finds: cones, flowers, leaves, twigs
- . glue gun and glue sticks
- . gluter
- . green faux sphagnum moss
- . moss cloth, 2' x 4'
- . wooden crate, 18"-square

✂ design tips:

- The more you distress the Birch Bark Project Paper, the more realistic it will look. You may also want to slightly "dirty" the paper by brushing a VERY diluted raw umber acrylic wash over it. You can create realistic-looking "bark curls" by rolling the glutered paper around your finger, then placing it in the desired position.

- If it needs support until it has dried, try using bits of aluminum foil to help it hold its shape and position.

INSTRUCTIONS

1. Distress the paper. Tear off all straight edges, then tear into workable 2"–4" pieces.

2. Dip one paper piece into gluter and place it on the crate, deliberately creating texture with wrinkles and wadding.

3. Continue with more paper pieces, leaving some of the crate showing. Allow some of the paper to extend into open areas and curl back on itself, simulating bark. Let dry overnight.

4. Hot-glue pieces of faux thin moss and lichen on random areas, gluing the moss along paths as though it had grown that way. Add your garden finds to the crate.

5. Cut thick moss into a 24" square (or an appropriate size for your crate) and hot-glue a tassel to each corner.

6. Drape the tablecloth over the table and set up your own private rendezvous between the garden chairs.

WOODLAND JUG

This fun and versatile little piece uses a papier-mâché wine jug filled with dried material. You could use the same technique on a watertight vessel as long as it did not have a very shiny surface, which would make it difficult for the wallpaper paste to adhere. You can always rough-up a shiny surface with coarse sandpaper.

design tips:

• The gray faux moss should be soft when you work with it. If it has been exposed to air and become dry and brittle, spritz it with a mist bottle full of warm water and tuck the pieces into a plastic bag overnight. They will be soft and pliable the next morning.

• You can make almost a "moss paste" with the above technique, and then you can put a very thin spread of this paste on your surface. Experiment with this; it really is an interesting technique that we have only begun to play with.

INSTRUCTIONS

1. Distress the paper and tear into small pieces, tearing off all straight edges.

2. Dip paper pieces into wallpaper paste and apply to the wine jug, overlapping pieces to entirely cover the surface. Let dry overnight.

3. Dip individual, small pieces of the gray moss into wallpaper paste, saturating it with the paste and working the paste through the moss.

4. Place the moss on the jug and press it as flat as possible. If necessary, add more paste. Vary the two moss colors as you work, sometimes blending them together with your fingers. Let the moss run in "veins" over the jug's surface. Let dry overnight.

5. Fill the jug with two or three interesting sticks.

MATERIALS

. 1 sheet Birch Bark Project Paper

. faux moss: gray, green

. interesting sticks

. papier-mâché wine jug

. premixed water-based wallpaper paste

CHAPTER FIVE

CHLOE'S CUPBOARD

"Just one more trinket, cheri, s'il vous plait."
Maybe it's because Chloe was born in Paris, but pretty
frivolous things just seem to gravitate to her. If there is a feather
boa or beaded purse within ten miles, it will find its way into Chloe's cupboard. Soft music (she is partial to light opera) and her favorite jasmine incense are
gentle notes in the background. Romantic and girlish things fill her small apartment; but instead
of looking cluttered, the effect is warm, cozy, and very inviting. She is one of those people who actually can
take flea-market finds and bits of this and that, and add paper, paste, and a liberal dash of imagination to
create a finished effect worthy of a magazine-style shot. A cast-off garage-sale lamp becomes a rose
petal concoction, throwing soft light on a floppy paper hat and a favorite antique image of a "Folies Ber-geres" girl. A camisole fashioned from paper that is actually made of silk vies for attention with a papier-mâché mannequin decked out in a "pretty in pink" ribbon-and-paper corset. Oh, and the cup-board? It was rescued from a past life of storing typing paper and file folders, and she picked it up for the bargain price of being willing to haul it away. If it is fun, frothy and fabulous, you will probably find it in Chloe's Cupboard.

ENGLISH ROSEBUD BOX

This is a very special little box that is just the right size for keeping special (and probably frivolous) things. I have one on my desk at work and it tends to collect stray seeds that friends bring in, a few theater mementos, three of my favorite pens, and not surprisingly, bits and scraps of special pieces of papers and trims that come my way.

MATERIALS

. 1 sheet red soft-textured paper

. 23 red faux rosebuds

. candle box

. faux green moss

. faux yellow rosebud

. glue gun and glue sticks

. paintbrush

. premixed water-based wallpaper paste

INSTRUCTIONS

1. Distress the paper and tear into workable 2"–3" pieces.

2. Paint a small portion of the box with the wallpaper paste and apply the paper. Continue until the box is covered, working small areas at a time. Cover all surfaces both inside and out. You may need to prop the lid open and allow some areas to dry before proceeding with the pasting. Let everything dry overnight.

3. Cut the stems off the rosebuds and discard stems or save for other uses.

4. Hot-glue the rosebuds onto the top of the lid, in three rows, eight buds in each row. Place the yellow bud near one end, not in the center.

5. Take small natural clumps of the faux moss and hot-glue them gently into all the spaces between the rosebuds.

6. Continue hot-gluing the moss around the perimeter of the lid, letting small bits of it flow over the side to give it a very lush look.

ROSE PETAL LAMP & LAMP SHADE

If you were to find this lamp in an exclusive boutique, it would easily cost $150–$300. Our lamp base was a very inexpensive one that we found in one of the outlet stores; but after we laminated on the Pink Cloud Handmade Paper, it looked like it was made of a pale pink stone. Use a regular lightbulb if you are looking for basic illumination or try one of the colored ones to add a very soft romantic glow to a room.

MATERIALS

. 1 sheet Pink Cloud Handmade Paper

. 10 faux burgundy rose petals

. 20' ribbon

. 30 faux pale green rose petals

. 200 faux pale pink rose petals

. glue gun and glue sticks

. lamp base

. liquid laminate

. paintbrush

. self-adhesive lamp shade, 4" x 10" x 8"

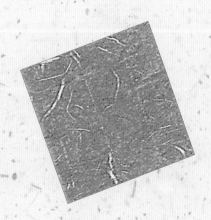

INSTRUCTIONS

1. Peel the protective cover off the lamp shade.

2. Starting at the bottom of the lamp shade, place one row of green faux rose petals along the bottom, letting two-thirds of each petal drop over the rim and overlapping each petal about ¼".

3. Place a row of pink faux rose petals above the row of pale green rose petals, with the tip of each pink petal over-lapping the tops of two green petals by about ¼". The pink petals should also overlap each other by about ¼".

4. Continue placing rows of pink petals in this way until you reach the top. It should take about 10 rows. The top row of petals should be extended about ¼" above the shade's rim. Tuck this overlap to the inside and hot-glue down.

5. Cut the ribbon into eight 11" pieces and hot-glue them evenly around the top rim of the shade, letting them gently fall down over the petals. Cut them to different lengths and softly knot some, leaving others straight.

6. Make rosebuds out of the burgundy rose petals by rolling each one into a cone shape and securing the bottom with a drop of hot glue. Cut small strips from green faux rose petals for leaves and hot-glue two to the bottom of the bud. Hot-glue one rosebud to each of the ribbons.

7. To cover the lamp base, tear the paper into workable-sized pieces, being certain to tear off any straight edges.

8. Brush the laminate onto the lamp base and apply the paper pieces, working small areas at a time and overlapping the edges of the papers. Let dry, then apply several finish coats to seal the lamp base, allowing each coat to dry between applications.

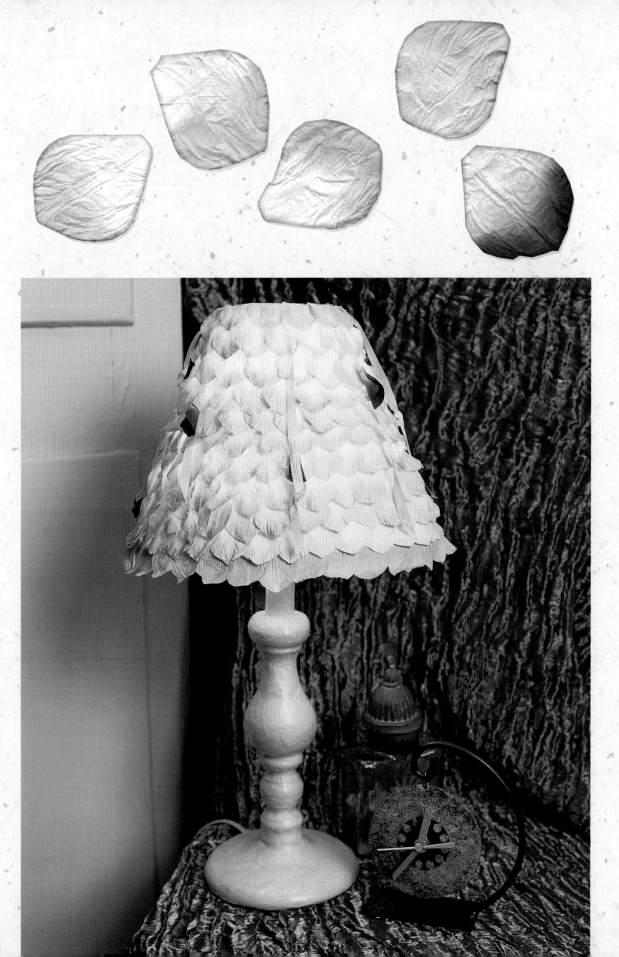

PAPER ROSE VASE

Our Paper Rose Vase has the look and patina of an old porcelain piece. You really have to touch the vase to realize that it is a papier-mâché base with a paper and paint technique on the surface. We chose to cut off the top of the vase form to create our desired look, but this is totally optional and would only depend on the shape that you wanted to have. We finished off our vignette with a small copper container of what appears to be real dried hydrangeas but are actually incredibly realistic look-alikes.

MATERIALS

. 2 garden finds for rose centers (we used the tops of poppy pods)

. 2 sheets milky coffee-colored paper

. acrylic paints: copper metallic, dark brown, pink, plum, rust

. acrylic sealer (optional)

. glue gun and glue sticks

. gluter

. paintbrushes

. pencil

. scissors

. sponge

. vase

INSTRUCTIONS

1. Cut top lip off the vase (optional).

2. Tear the paper into 3"–4" pieces. Cover the surface of the vase with the torn pieces by dipping them into gluter, skimming off excess with fingers and applying and overlapping the papers, covering the torn top edge. Let dry overnight.

3. From the paper, cut about 36 "U" shapes with slightly flared bottoms for the rose petals and about 10 elongated ovals for the leaves.

4. Brush the entire vase with a watered-down pink acrylic paint and let dry.

5. Paint the inside of vase with undiluted pink paint.

6. Lightly draw rose vines around the vase, then paint them with dark brown paint.

7. For the roses, dip five large petals in gluter and place them in a circle on the side of the vase. Curl and shape the edges and press them flat. Place four smaller petals on top. Glue, press and shape unevenly. Let dry. Hot-glue "garden find" for center.

8. For the rosebuds, roll two petals together in a cone shape. Press and shape these onto the vase surface, placing them near the end of the painted vines. Let dry.

9. Paint roses pink, with highlights of plum and rust.

10. Drizzle watered-down paint over the vase, layering colors and sponging as you go. Let dry. Apply more as desired.

11. Add a little copper metallic paint, but sponge most of it away for a vintage look.

12. If desired, seal with an acrylic sealer in a finish that will complement your look.

FRENCH DRIED HYDRANGEAS IN COPPER CONTAINER

MATERIALS

. 1 Cornflower & Rose Smoke French
   Dried Hydrangea

. floral foam block

  glue gun and glue sticks

. medium copper cake pan

. scissors

INSTRUCTIONS

1. Cut the floral foam to fit the bottom of the cake pan and level with the top of the pan.

2. Hot-glue the foam in place.

3. Separate the individual flowerets on the hydrangea and insert them into the floral foam, starting at the center and working out to the edges. As you work toward the outer edges, slightly slant your flowers outward so that by the time you place the last perimeter flowerets into the foam, some of the "petals" will overlap the sides.

PAPER CABBAGE ROSE VINE

When it comes to creating a romantic look, nothing beats large full-blown cabbage roses. We have created ours with handmade paper, individually painted, then put together on a paper-covered wire that has a very natural appearance without the annoying factor of thorns. Use your Cabbage Rose Vine along a stair banister, around a picture frame or window, or do as we did and let it meander over the top of an antique birdcage, sans bird—instant romance!

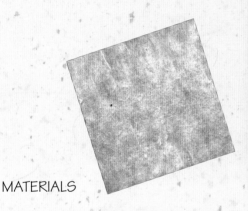

MATERIALS

. 2 sheets milky coffee-colored paper

. 12' mauve paper-covered wire

. acrylic paints: greens, mauve, pinks

. bamboo skewer

. gluter

. paintbrushes

. paper towels

. photocopier

. scissors

INSTRUCTIONS

1. Distress the paper.

2. Photocopy the Petal Pattern on page 59. Cut 15 rose petals in various sizes, large petals 2½" x 3" and small petals 2" x 2½".

3. Photocopy the Leaf Pattern on page 59. Cut 10 rose leaves, about 1" x 2".

4. Paint rose petals pink, fading into the mauve at the bottom. Smaller petals should be a bit darker than the large petals. Paint both sides and place them on a paper towel to dry (see design tip on page 59).

5. Paint the rose leaves with the two colors of green, varying the shades to give them a more natural appearance and place them on a paper towel to dry.

6. To assemble the rose, first roll one of the small petals into a cone and pinch it together at the bottom.

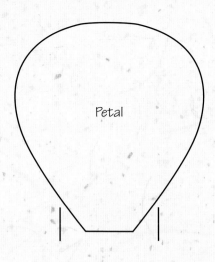

Petal

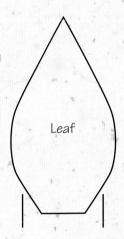

Leaf

ABOVE: Petal and Leaf Patterns
(enlarge or reduce as desired)

design tip:

• When painting our rose petals, we deliberately gave them an uneven, almost "splotchy" appearance, achieved by varying the amount of paint on any given part of a petal. This gave our roses a very antiqued look with an almost velvety patina.

7. Paint the next petal with the gluter and wrap it around the first petal, overlapping at the bottom of the rose. Continue wrapping the petals and vary where you overlap them at the bottom. Put about five or six more small petals on.

8. Using the same process, start placing the larger petals on the flower. Stagger the overlap at the bottom and pinch them tightly together.

9. When all the petals are secure, glue one leaf to the underside of the rose, anchoring and curling it up the petal. Repeat with another petal on the opposite side.

10. Glue a third leaf to the others and wrap it around the paper-covered wire attaching the rose to the wire. Add more leaves, either single or double to the paper-covered wire at random intervals. Let dry overnight.

11. When the roses are dry, curl the petals under, using a bamboo skewer. Give the smaller petal very tight curls and the larger ones looser, slightly curved curls.

12. Curl the tops of the leaves out.

FEMALE TORSO WITH PAPER CORSET

Sexy and demure at the same time, this is one of Chloe's favorite pieces. She had always loved old mannequins and hoped to find one at a bargain price, maybe left in an old department store's dusty basement or perhaps at a Paris flea market. This piece has just the look she was after; and for those of you who don't sew, you can even use a glue gun for the seams.

MATERIALS

CORSET

. 1 package variegated silk ribbon, ¼" x 20'

. 1 package variegated silk ribbon, ½" x 20'

. 1 package grommets

. 1 package stocking garters

. 1 sheet French Lace Paper

. 1 sheet Peppermint Quilt Paper

. 1 yard iron-on interfacing

. glue gun and glue sticks

. iron

. miniature corset pattern

. photocopier

. scissors

. sewing machine

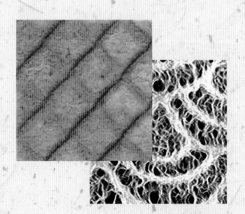

INSTRUCTIONS

CORSET

1. Photocopy Corset Patterns on page 62.

2. Iron the interfacing to the wrong side of the Peppermint paper.

3. Cut the corset pattern from the interfaced paper, taking care that the print on the paper is running in the same direction.

4. With right sides together, sew all the sides together except the center front.

5. Fold the center pieces on the folding line to the back of the corset and press in place.

6. Hot-glue them to the interfacing.

7. Fold the top edge ½" down all the way around the corset top and hot-glue to the interfacing.

8. Put seven grommets, evenly spaced, ½" from the center edge down each side of the center front of the corset.

9. Leaving a ½" extra at the top and 1" at the bottom, hot-glue the ¼" ribbon down each seam on the corset, to accent the shape. Fold the extra top ½" to the inside and hot-glue to the interfacing. Leave a 1" piece at the bottom and trim to a point.

10. Hand-tear the French Lace paper along the scallops and glue to the underside of the top and bottom of the corset so it peeks over the edges, making a lace trim.

11. Attach the garters with the ½" ribbon to the bottom of the corset at the two front and two back seams and hot-glue the ribbons into place.

12. Lace the ¼" ribbon through the grommets and tie a soft bow at the top.

MATERIALS

TORSO

. 1 papier-mâché female torso,
  22½" x 10½"

. 1 piece variegated ribbon, ½" x 24"

. 2 sheets dusty plum soft-textured
  paper

. gluter

INSTRUCTIONS

TORSO

1.   Tear the paper into workable 2"–4" pieces.

2.   Dip into the gluter and apply to the torso, allowing paper
     to overlap. Cover completely and let dry.

3.   Tie a piece of the ribbon around the neck and cut to fit,
     for a simple choker.

4.   Dress with the corset.

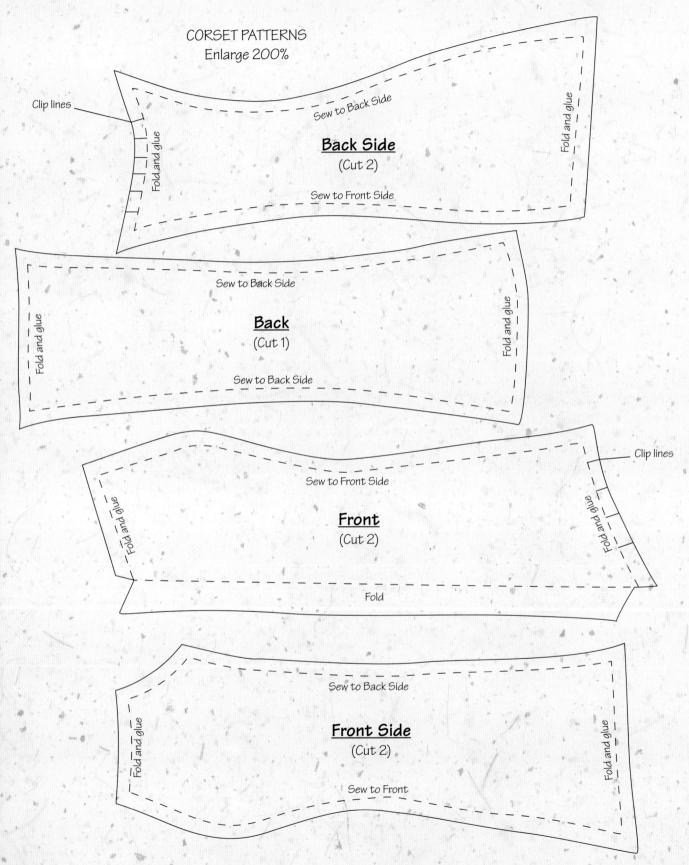

CORSET PATTERNS
Enlarge 200%

Clip lines

Sew to Back Side

Fold and glue

Back Side
(Cut 2)

Fold and glue

Sew to Front Side

Sew to Back Side

Fold and glue

Back
(Cut 1)

Fold and glue

Sew to Back Side

Sew to Front Side

Clip lines

Fold and glue

Front
(Cut 2)

Fold and glue

Fold

Sew to Back Side

Fold and glue

Front Side
(Cut 2)

Fold and glue

Sew to Front

 design tip:

- A smaller version of this with just one heart shell, either a "valentine" or a "pudgy," would make a delightful token of your affection for a special someone.

HEART SEASHELL SHADOW BOX

It's difficult to believe that these are actually real shells, but they are. Wouldn't you just love to know the little fellows who chose to live in a valentine? They are so cute we felt they really deserved a special presentation of their own—in red, of course!

MATERIALS

. 1 sheet red handmade paper

. 2 pudgy heart shells

. 3 valentine heart shells

. glue gun and glue sticks

. paintbrush

. premixed water-based wallpaper paste

. shadow frame

. sponge

INSTRUCTIONS

1. Tear the paper into small workable pieces, being sure to tear off any straight edges.

2. Paint the wallpaper paste onto the shadow frame, small areas at a time, and paste the paper down, working it flat with a sponge or fingertips. Start with the inside and outside edges, leaving the front face of the frame and the large inside back area for last. This will allow you to cover any awkward edges and give the most visible parts a smooth appearance. Cover the frame completely on front and around sides to back edge. Allow to dry overnight.

3. When completely dry, hot-glue the three valentine shells to the inside top and position the two pudgy shells underneath and stagger between the top ones.

4. If desired, you could seal the paper before adding the shells, but the wallpaper paste actually finishes with a soft sheen.

FRENCH CAMISOLE

We used a very simple, commercially available pattern for our French Camisole, then executed it in the most gossamer of papers. Even when you touch it, you will have a difficult time believing that this is paper. Handmade entirely of silk fibers, the Spun Silk Papers have the ethereal delicacy associated with fine fabric. This particular "Montage" selection has an array of visible colored fibers lacing through the surface.

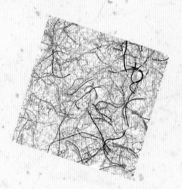

MATERIALS

. 1 package variegated silk ribbon

. 2 sheets Lilac Montage Spun Silk Paper

. needle and thread

. scissors

. sewing machine

. simple camisole pattern

design tip:

• This is a very inexpensive piece of wall art that will give a romantic, feminine touch to your bedroom or, if you are fortunate enough to have one, a separate powder room.

INSTRUCTIONS

1. Cut camisole pattern out of the paper.

2. Sew as instructed by the pattern directions.

3. Instead of making the straps from the paper, cut long lengths of ribbon and hand-stitch them to the paper camisole. Tie soft bows at the top of the shoulder and let the ends drape down.

4. Make three small rosebuds from the ribbon by rolling it into a cone shape and affixing with several hand-stitches, then affix these to the shirt front with several more hand-stitches.

CHORUS GIRL WALL ART

The European postcards of the early twentieth century frequently celebrated female dancers in elaborate fantasy-inspired and often sensual costumes. Always tasteful, the early "French" postcards were avidly sought and collected, and even today the artwork and color achieved by the German and French lithographers amaze us.

Chloe keeps this, her favorite one, in her cupboard along with her collection of ostrich plumage.

INSTRUCTIONS

MATERIALS

. 3 sheets handmade paper: hunter green, pine green, mustard yellow

. acrylic sealer with matte finish (optional)

. chorus girl image

. premixed water-based wallpaper paste

. sponge brush

. Styrofoam board, 7" x 10" x 1"

1. Cut a piece of mustard yellow paper about 2" larger than the board. Apply the paste to the Styrofoam board and place the paper on top, working all the air bubbles out to the sides. Apply more paste to the edges of the paper and wrap them around the sides and onto the back of the board.

2. On the back side of the pine green and hunter green papers, measure and mark each piece to be approximately ½" smaller than the piece beneath it, making the pine piece larger than the hunter.

3. Tear the pine green and the hunter green papers along the fold lines. Paste down first the pine, then the hunter.

4. Distress the image gently, then hand-press flat.

5. Tear the edges of the image to size it so that approximately ½" of the hunter green paper will be exposed.

6. Apply the paste to the back of the image. Apply the center of the image first and work the wrinkles and air bubbles out to the sides.

7. Let dry. Apply matte acrylic sealer if desired.

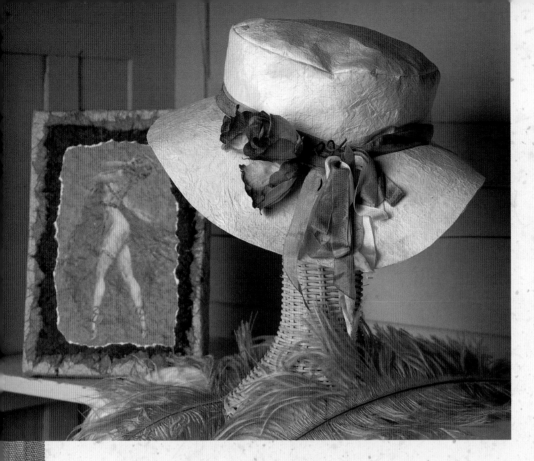

CHLOE'S GARDEN HAT

Chloe never goes out to work in her tiny patio garden without her favorite floppy garden hat. A bright sunshiny yellow, it makes her feel happy just to look at it, which she does frequently. Perched on a rattan mannequin head nestled into a corner of her cupboard with ostrich plumes and a "Folies Bergeres" image, it doubles as an article of interest.

MATERIALS

. 1 package variegated silk ribbon in spring colors

. 2 sheets Sunflower Paper

. 3 red and yellow faux rosebuds

. glue gun and glue sticks

. hat pattern with a medium-sized brim and a small classic crown

. heavy-duty iron-on interfacing

. iron

. iron-on fusible webbing

. scissors

. sewing machine

INSTRUCTIONS

1. Cut hat pattern out of the paper.

2. On the wrong side of the paper, iron on the heavy-duty interfacing to the crown, top of hat, and one of the brims.

3. On the other brim, on the wrong side of the paper, iron on fusible webbing.

4. Following the pattern instructions, put the wrong sides of the two brims together and iron to fuse, giving you two (upper and lower) finished sides to your brim.

5. Continue pattern directions and sew the crown together at the back. With right sides together, sew the top of the hat to the crown, clipping all edges on seam allowance and press to inside of the hat.

6. Turn hat and with right sides together, sew the brim onto the crown, again clipping edges and pressing.

7. Tie the ribbon into a soft, "loopy" bow and hot-glue it to the brim. Clip ribbon ends to various lengths.

8. Hot-glue three faux rosebuds into nest of ribbon loops.

CHLOE'S EVENING BAG

This little bag is actually strong enough that you could use it occasionally to hold a lipstick and car keys for a special evening out. We made ours to hang in the studio, where we tuck all those little bits of ribbon, beads, and trim that seem to get lost otherwise.

MATERIALS

. 1 sheet mauve soft-textured paper

. 1 yard iron-on pellon facing

. glue gun and glue sticks

. iron

. make generic antiqued beaded fringe

. needle and thread

. scissors

. sewing machine

. Velcro dots

design tip:

• IMPORTANT: You MUST apply a small bit of hot glue to fringe where you want to cut it to keep it from unraveling.

INSTRUCTIONS

1. Cut two 8½" x 7½" rectangles from the paper. Trim bottom corners off, rounding them for a "U"-shaped bag.

2. Iron on the pellon lining to the back side of the paper bag pieces and trim to fit.

3. To add the bottom fringe, hand-stitch the fringe to the right side of one of the bag pieces. Start at the top of one side and stitch along edge to other side.

4. With right sides together, machine-stitch the two sides together, then gently turn the bag right side out.

5. Fold the top edge down 1" and hot-glue to the inside of bag. Hot-glue Velcro dots to the inside center of the bag to make a closure.

6. Hot-glue a row of fringe around the top outside of the bag. Hot-glue a second row 2" below the first .

7. Unstring some of the leftover fringe, then re-string the beads to create the handle.

PERSONAL PARTY LITES

Unlike her older sister Chloe, Sasha is NOT a "stay at home and read a book" kind of genteel lady. She's a party girl and loves nothing better than to put on her high-heeled slippers, and her favorite swirly silk dress (actually made of paper) to head for the music (she cuts a mean salsa). A big believer in "I could have danced all night," she is seldom willing to quit before the band does, though she has been known to overdo it and simply collapse in the chandelier.

And what about all those fabulous little lights in the background? Well, actually they are a **loose ends** exclusive that we have carried for years, called Jardin Party Lites. But we have had so many people ask about how to make them that we thought we might as well take one apart and give you the pattern so that you can make your own Personal Party Lites. The amount of paper that you will need will be based on a number of factors including how many color combinations you want to do, how many lights are on the strands you buy, etc. So, we are listing just one sheet each of the colors that are similar to the ones on our 50-light strand.

RIGHT: Try draping several strands of Personal Party Lites together for a more festive look.

68

MATERIALS

. 1 sheet Persimmon Quilt Paper

. 6 sheets patterned handmade paper in various colors

. glue stick

. photocopier

. scissors

. strand of small Christmas lights

design tip:

• These can add a magical glow to a dinner party.

INSTRUCTIONS

1. Photocopy the Party Lite Pattern.

2. Cut out various colors combinations of the two pattern pieces from the patterned papers, enough to cover as many lights as you have on your strand.

3. Glue the rim onto the hat, allowing the rim to overlap approximately ¼".

4. Roll the hats into cone shapes, securing the open sides with the glue stick.

5. Gently ease the hats onto your lights, making a small clip or two if necessary to allow the paper to slip on easily. You want it to fit snugly, however, so that the paper does not easily fall off.

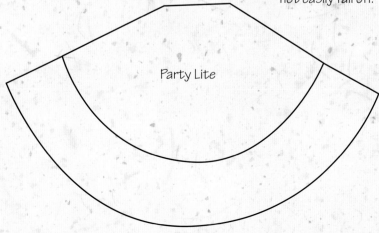

Party Lite

LEFT: Party Lite Pattern (actual size)

69

CHANDELIER LAMP SHADES

One of our absolute favorite things to find are old lighting fixtures. There are so many fun things you can do with them. This one was designed for candles, so we created a "faux fixture" that looks great hanging over our design library corner (yes, Sasha is perched up there, too). We made our supply list for four shades since one place would be occupied by a pear—obviously you would want to increase or decrease the supplies based on how many shades you want for your chandelier. We used short pillar candles to support our lamp shades (these are for looks and support only and they would not be fire safe). You could also make your own pillars using the core inside paper towels, etc., and cut to length; but you would want to cover them with a neutral paper first to simulate the look of a candle.

MATERIALS

. 1 sheet purple soft-textured paper

. 1 sheet Persimmon Quilt Paper

. 2 sheets handmade paper: mustard
  yellow, pine green

. 4 pillar candles, 2" x 4"

. 4 small lamp shades, 4" x 3" x 4"

. aged candle chandelier

. faux pear

. glue stick

. pencil

. scissors

INSTRUCTIONS

1. Mark cut lines for four lamp shade covers by rolling each
   lamp shade across a piece of paper and marking the path
   with a pencil about 1" below the bottom edge of the shade,
   then rolling the shade back the other way and marking
   the path about 1" above the top edge of the shade.

2. Cut a lamp shade cover from each sheet of paper.

3. Wrap paper cover around the lamp shade and glue the
   back seam into place.

4. Trim the top and bottom edges to ¾"
   above the rims and glue them to the
   inside of the shades. Let dry.

5. Anchor the candles onto the four candle
   spikes. Place the shades on the candles.

6. Place the pear on the fifth candle spike.

✂ design tips:

• This is such a quick and easy project that you
could make an assortment of different paper
shades, maybe some with printed designs or
oriental script or geometric patterns or old
sheet music, or, or, or . . .

• If that looks like an orange to you in our
Chandelier, you're right. We liked the pear so
much that we decided to tuck an orange in too!

CHAPTER SIX

VICTORIA'S VERANDA

It's actually more like a deck than a classical veranda. Victoria would prefer to call this the "piazza," but knows that is probably a bit much. Extending off her bedroom, this small corner of private space is where, weather permitting, Victoria loves to spend a summer afternoon sipping lemon-flavored tea and reading a mystery or romance novel. Fantasy has a prominent role in her imaginative life, and she surrounds herself with things that help her play her chosen role.

PARISIAN WOMEN LAMP

This is a really beautiful lamp when it is lit with a low-wattage bulb. We consider this to be a "four hand" project because you are working with a full sheet of paper (not small pieces), making it rather awkward to handle with the laminate on it. Find an artsy friend to help, and you will find it infinitely easier.

MATERIALS

. 1 beach glass compote

. 1 sheet Parisian Women Project Paper

. antiqued beaded generic fringe

. drill and bits for drilling glass

. duct tape

. glue gun and glue sticks

. jar adapter lamp fitting

. liquid laminate

. paintbrush

. scissors

INSTRUCTIONS

1. If you are going to drill the hole yourself, you will need to place a piece of duct tape at the spot where you want to drill (this will help keep it from cracking). If the glass is thick where you want to make the hole, it is better to work with the smallest bit and gradually build up to the ¼" bit size.

2. If you do not want to drill the hole yourself, a glass shop will do this for you.

3. Distress the paper and cut a 14" x 21½" piece.

4. Brush the back of the paper with the laminate and, with the help of a friend, wrap it evenly around the compote. Press the paper into the curves on the compote, working them until you have the paper as smooth as possible. There will be some wrinkles, but just work them flat on the glass surface.

5. Trim the top and bottom, making a hole in the paper where you have drilled. After letting it dry between coats, give the compote 2–3 more coats of the laminate.

6. Cut two 22" pieces of fringe. Hot-glue one piece to the top outside of the compote, and the other to the inside.

7. Place a jar adapter lamp fitting in the bottom of the compote and string the cord through the hole drilled in the bottom. You will have to reattach the plug.

PARISIAN WOMEN BOUDOIR CHAIR

You will feel special sitting on this VERY feminine chair. Although it is quite usable, it is particularly wonderful placed near a table scattered with a vase of flowers, a romantic novel, something cool to sip on, or a few special trinkets. A charming companion, (especially a furry one) is the perfect complement. This is a "just because" chair, one of those rare creatures that needs no justification for its existence besides its beauty.

MATERIALS

SKIRT AND CHAIR

. 1 yard batting

. 1½ yards unbleached muslin

. 3 sheets sage soft-textured paper

. 3 yards Guava Silk Shimmer Fabric

. 4 yards iron-on adhesive

. 10' roll antiqued beaded fringe

. 20' roll Parisian Women Project Paper

. acrylic paints: burnt umber, gold, olive green

. bentwood side chair

. glue gun and glue sticks

. gluter

. iron

. paintbrushes

. ruler

. scissors

. sewing machine and thread

. sponge

. staple gun and staples

. straight pins

. Velcro tape or dots

INSTRUCTIONS

SKIRT

1. Cut 14' length of Parisian Women paper. Distress and hand-press flat.

2. Water down the paint colors (about 2:1 water and paint). If desired, mix the paints together for a muddier color.

3. Antique the paper with the watered-down paint and sponge most of it off. Let dry to see the effect. If desired, repeat the process.

4. When dry, iron the iron-on adhesive to the back side of the paper. Peel off the protective cover and iron on the Silk Shimmer fabric.

5. Cut four 24"-long panels from the antiqued Parisian Women paper, starting at the top with the beaded-fringe pattern and ending at the bottom 6" below the top of the beaded fringe pattern (top of trim).

6. With the patterned surfaces of the paper facing each other, sew one side of each panel to one side of another panel, so that the beaded-fringe pattern matches up.

7. Iron 1" pleats at the top of the skirt, and machine-stitch in place by running one long topstitch about ½" from the top and the entire length of the skirt.

8. Set skirt aside.

9. Cut a 22" square from the unbleached muslin and a 22" square from the Silk Shimmer fabric, then cut both into 19"-diameter circles.

10. Baste the two circles together, forming the seat cover.

11. Pin three panels of the top of the skirt around the perimeter of the seat cover, but leave the fourth panel free for the back of the chair.

12. Stitch in place.

13. Attach a small piece of Velcro to the inside top of the free panel, and one piece to the outside of the opposite side of the skirt, making your closure.

14. Fold down the raw edge of the free panel, and hot-glue to the inside.

15. Fold under a 2" hem at the bottom of the skirt. Press in place and hot-glue.

16. Hot-glue the antiqued beaded fringe around the edge where the skirt joins the seat cover.

CHAIR

1. Remove the seat and set aside.

2. Tear soft-textured paper into workable 2"–3" pieces, and dip them into the gluter, covering the chair with the paper, allowing the pieces to overlap. Let dry overnight.

3. Cut a 12" x 19" piece of the painted Parisian Women paper so that the beaded fringe pattern is about 3"–4" from the top.

4. Fold ¼" at the top and bottom to the inside and hot-glue down the two raw edges.

5. Place this piece on your chair back and hot-gluing one side at a time, tuck and roll the sides around to the back, pulling the second side taut.

6. Hot-glue a piece of the beaded fringe over the beaded-fringe pattern.

7. Cut a 24" square from batting and staple edges to the underside of the seat.

8. Cut a 24" square from unbleached muslin. Place it over the batting and staple it to the underside of the seat. Trim the batting and muslin edges.

9. Reattach the seat to the chair.

10. Place the skirt and seat cover on the chair.

11. Tear two 8"-wide strips from Silk Shimmer fabric sand selvage to selvage (about 44"), and tie two big, floppy bows to the back of the chair.

design tip:

• To make our pillow, simply follow the general instructions for the Wild Things Paper Pillows on page 22, substituting the Parisian Women Project Paper. For contrast we didn't "paint down" the paper for the pillow. After stuffing the pillow, we tore four long strips of Silk Shimmer "Gold" and tied them into bows for the four corners.

FIFI FLOOR MAT

This floor mat starts out with a commercially available canvas mat already cut to size and ready to be turned into a custom creation. We found ours at our local art store, but many craft stores also carry them. Because Victoria is such a romantic, we chose an early twentieth-century French postcard image, then took it to a print shop and had it enlarged on a color copier. Remember that color images must be done on a heat-setting machine (commercial color copiers, etc.), otherwise colors will run.

MATERIALS

. 1 sheet hunter green soft-textured paper

. 2 sheets Buttercup Spun Silk Paper

. acrylic sealer

. canvas mat, 23¼" x 34"

. premixed water-based wallpaper paste

. scissors

. sponge brushes

. sponges

. vintage image, enlarged to 10½" x 16¼"

INSTRUCTIONS

1. Apply wallpaper paste to one-third of the canvas mat and gently ease the Spun Silk paper onto the paste, starting at one end and spreading it flat with your hands, working out the wrinkles and bubbles as you go.

2. Do the same with the next one-third of the canvas, working the paper gently down.

3. To finish the last section, you will need to splice a second piece of Spun Silk paper onto the first. Be certain to tear, not cut, the edge that will splice with the first piece. The torn edges will easily blend into each other and be almost invisible. Let dry thoroughly (usually overnight).

4. Tear a 4" x 23½" strip and a 4" x 34" strip of the soft-textured paper. Fold them lengthwise down the center. Crease the fold sharply, using fingernail, or run the flat side of a blade down the fold. Dampen the fold line with a wet finger, then easily tear along fold. Cut the strips to required length.

5. To create a 2" border around the edge of your mat, apply wallpaper paste along a 2" strip on one of the 34" long sides of your mat and place the 2" fold area of soft-textured paper onto the pasted strip. Do the same on the other 34" side. Trim off any excess within ½", turn mat over and paste the bottom 2" in place on back side.

6. Repeat for the 23½" sides, again trimming the ends to within ½" and making square corners as you turn the remaining 2" sides to the back and paste down. Clean up excess paste with a slightly dampened sponge.

7. Coat the back of your enlarged image with the wallpaper paste. Center it on the mat, and working from the middle out, smooth out wrinkles and air bubbles with your fingertips or a dry sponge. Clean any excess paste up with a slightly dampened sponge. Let dry overnight.

8. Give your finished mat at least five coats of acrylic sealer. We found it easiest to use a sponge brush, applying gently to avoid bubbles and foaming (which can occur if you brush too vigorously).

9. With five coats of sealer, your floor mat will stand up to a moderate amount of foot traffic, but it is best to use it in an area that will not see heavy use. It is also quite wonderful tacked up on a wall!

design tip:

• We have found the canvas mats that are available at art/craft stores to also be perfect for creating wall art. The technique is exactly the same; but rather than using them as a rug, we took three that we made with old images of food and food-related items from the 1930s and put them on a kitchen wall to tell a story. Usually, three coats of acrylic sealer are sufficient if you are not going to be walking on the pieces.

PARISIAN WOMEN TEA CHEST

A place to keep special things, this is one of Chloe's favorite pieces. Here, she tucks in her ribbon-tied packet of love letters, her favorite frangipani incense, an eclectic collection of small buttons and trinkets, some favorite snippets of handmade paper, a close-at-hand supply of a few herbal teabags and, of course, her journal.

This tin chest is a great place for whatever you like to keep private and close by.

MATERIALS

. 1 sheet Silver Metallic Wash Project Paper

. 2 sheets Parisian Women Project Paper

. acrylic paints: brown, mustard yellow, olive green

. liquid laminate

. medium French Tin Tea Chest

. paintbrushes

. scissors

. sponge

design tip:
• If you're really ambitious, you can find chests or boxes that come in a set and cover each one a little bit differently.

INSTRUCTIONS

1. Distress the Parisian Women paper and hand-press flat.

2. For an antique finish, water down the paints (about 3:1 water and paint), and dab them on the paper. Using a damp sponge, wipe off most of the paint. Let dry and repeat until you have the desired effect. Let paper dry completely.

3. Choose part of the pattern for the top of chest and cut to 8½" x 11". Apply laminate to the back of the paper and adhere to the top. The paper should cover the top and extend about 1½" down the curve. Give the paper another coat of laminate on the top.

4. To add the bead design on the four sides of the lid, cut two 9" x 3" pieces, starting at the top of the black tape design. Adhere these two pieces to the two shorter sides of the lid, letting it overlap your top piece by ½". Do the same for the front and back sides of the lid, cutting two 12½" x 3" pieces and trimming the corners to fit. Add another coat of laminate to these pieces.

5. Distress the Silver paper and tear into 3"–4" pieces, being certain to tear off all straight edges.

6. Adhere this paper to the inside of the lid and the collar of the chest, allowing the pieces to overlap each other.

7. Cut two 13" x 4" pieces of the Parisian Women paper and adhere to the front and back bottom side of the chest, letting them slightly overlap the edges.

8. Cut two more 4" x 9" pieces of the Parisian Women paper and adhere to the shorter ends of the chest. They should slightly overlap to the bottom of the chest but fit just to the side corners. Give these bottom side pieces another coat of laminate.

9. Give the chest 2–3 more coats of laminate. Let dry between coats.

 design tip:

- If you want to add a bit more "ooh la la" to the chest, you can cut some of the ladies out of the Parisian Women Project Paper and laminate the individual images onto the Silver Metallic Wash Project Paper on the inside of the lid!

79

WILDFLOWER ANTIQUE WINDOW

Everybody has that thing that just does it for them. For some, it's garage sales, and for others, it's fabulous food or fine wine. For me it's architectural salvage. I mean, you give me a line on some old doors and windows and I am gone! Art doesn't always share my unbridled enthusiasm for these treasures and there have been times when I had to consider whether I wanted more doors and windows or whether I wanted to stay married. But there is such a sense of "tales to be told" clinging to these discarded bones of our buildings and homes. Many need a bit of help before they can be reincarnated into their new life; but others are perfect, just as is, even with their peeling paint and missing panes.

You can use commercially available pressed flowers for this project, but we think half the fun is finding and pressing your own. Pansies are great, but look for those undiscovered "wallflowers" either in your yard or along the roadside. There's something about imperfectly pressed weeds, wildflowers, and even garden blooms, that seems to hit the right note with these old windows.

MATERIALS

. 2 sheets Dark Vanilla Spun Silk Paper

. 4 egg whites

. acrylic sealer (optional)

. multipaned window

. pressed florals

. sponge brush

INSTRUCTIONS

1. Repair and clean window if necessary.

2. Cut the paper to fit the panes of the window and set aside.

3. Brush egg white onto one pane, being careful not to foam up the egg white.

4. Arrange the flowers right side down on top of the egg white. The egg white will stay wet for about 10 minutes, allowing you to move the blooms around a bit if necessary.

5. Repeat the procedure on each pane, then let all panes dry for about 20 minutes.

6. Gently brush on a second coat of egg white, covering the backs of the flowers and all exposed areas, then cover with the Spun Silk paper and let dry.

7. Cover the paper with a coat of egg white and let dry.

8. If you are going to hang your window as a piece of artwork or in front of a real window as a sun catcher, this finish is enough. However, if you are going to use your window where it might get a bit more "wear and tear" (room divider, coffee tabletop, etc.), you can also seal the back with an acrylic sealer for more protection.

✂ design tip:
- Old windows are frequently missing glass panes. Of course, you can replace them, but consider leaving them out— they can add an interesting dimension of "negative space" where you can hang other goodies (like a small dried wildflower bouquet) in the empty spot. Also, these spaces provide for the possibility of interesting and unexpected framed "vistas" that now become part of your piece.

SPUN SILK "POTPOURRI" HANDMADE PAPER

Although we call this paper, it actually has no cellulose fiber in it at all. All of our Spun Silk papers are produced from the raw silk clots that are left by a specific type of moth that feeds on the leaves of the mulberry tree. Much handmade paper is made with the fibers of the mulberry tree. Maybe the moths are just making their own version? These look and feel more like a fine fabric than paper, and the Spun Silk sheets are especially beautiful with the various colors and types of threads scattered throughout.

We use this paper collection when we want transparent color, and with the wildflowers used in our window, we loved the way the threads picked up the same hues.

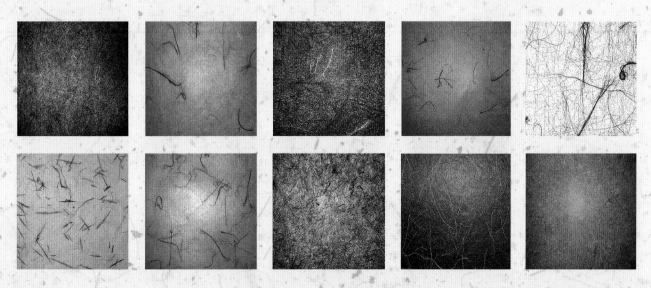

FRENCH PETROL CAN

And there, with its fruit gently swinging in the afternoon breeze, was the Pitcher Tree, long thought to be only a myth. Finding this fabled botanical was considered to be an occasion of great good fortune. It was believed that she who discovered it would be assured of a long and prosperous life; but should she try to return to this place, she would find only a plain tree.

The inspiration for this project came from a small park at which Art and I happened to stop to eat our lunch two years ago when we were driving from Frankfurt, Germany, down to Bavaria to work with one of our vendors. It looked like any woodland park until we began to walk along one of the paths; and there, tucked into private places, were bits of artwork, fragments of whimsy and small surprises. One of our favorites had apple wine pitchers for the annual fest hanging from the branches of an apple tree.

82

We loved the look and for our version, we used various sizes of these wonderful French Petrol Cans, actually used for transporting the same in Bangladesh. No petrol cans? No problem! Any lightweight pitcher would work equally well. You could also do an inside version of this if you have an open-beamed ceiling or overhead rack. Think dried floral materials, silk or paper flowers, or maybe garlic braids and faux veggies in a kitchen.

We used seven different sizes of our Tin Petrol Cans for our Pitcher Tree. Consider picking up small juice pitchers, creamers, etc., at yard sales for a very fun look. You can also buy transparent plastic water pitchers very inexpensively at discount stores during the summer. Because they are transparent, they will give an entirely different look to the finished project; and if hung outside, they will be translucent with the natural light.

Our directions are for just one Petrol Can; but as you can see, we made a few more in other color combinations. Although you could use a heavier paper for this project, we found the tissue weight to be ideal. As you slightly overlap the various shades of complementary colors, you will get other colors resulting from the translucency of the color combinations.

We worked with three different colors: greens, blues, and red/oranges. Metallic wash tissues also look great, especially if you apply a bit of drizzled metallic acrylic paint over the finished item.

MATERIALS

- . 3 sheets tissue papers: tangerine, burgundy, cranberry
- . 5-liter French Petrol Can
- . liquid laminate
- . paintbrush

INSTRUCTIONS

1. Distress the papers and tear all straight edges away.

2. Tear the papers into workable 2"–3" pieces.

3. Brush a layer of laminate on the can and apply the tissue randomly. Work in small areas.

4. Brush laminate over the pieces as you apply them and continue until the can is covered. It should resemble a crazy quilt.

5. Apply a final finish coat of laminate to give a soft sheen to the surface. (Additional coats of laminate will make the piece shinier.)

Reality Reminder:
You can't depend on your eyes when your imagination is out of focus.

—Unknown

CHAPTER SEVEN

RETRO ROOM

Sometimes it is
the materials you are surrounded with that demand to be
turned into something fun. And so
it was with Retro Room—actually
it's really more like a "Retro Corner,"
but that just doesn't have the
same panache. A collection of our
papers was just screaming for us
to do some-thing with them, when
this cast-off chest of drawers
showed up (yep, a garage sale
goodie). It seemed like the perfect
palette for showing off these
beautiful, hand-painted,

handmade papers. Naturally the thing couldn't just stand there all by itself, so a lamp and a wall clock seemed just the thing to complete the look. And where better to show off the look than in front of a cast-off vintage French door?

When shopping for papers for this type of collection, you want to find designs that repeat a theme, graphics or colors. Papers can impart a feeling that makes them work together without actually using the same colors or line configurations. I find that frequently the papers themselves will present their own suggestions, and you just have to be willing to listen.

RETRO LAMP

We found our lamp base at a large discount store for under $10. The self-adhesive lamp shades are usually available at most craft stores; and when you peel off the protective paper covering, that becomes your pattern. If you are using a regular lamp shade, you can easily make your own pattern by laying the shade on its side on your paper, then marking the path with a pencil about 1" from the shade's bottom edge while rolling it. Reverse the roll and do the same thing for the top edge. This doesn't have to be exact since you will turn the excess to the inside.

MATERIALS

. 1 sheet each Parisian Apartment Wallpapers: Ink Interlude, Spots

. glue gun and glue sticks

. liquid laminate

. paintbrush

. scissors

. self-adhesive lamp shade

. small lamp base

INSTRUCTIONS

LAMP BASE

1. Tear Spots paper into workable 2"–3" pieces, taking care to leave the spots intact.

2. Paint a small area on the lamp base with the laminate and apply the paper. Continue adding paper, overlapping edges but keeping the spots intact until the lamp is covered.

3. Paint several coats of the laminate over the papers, allowing the laminate to dry between applications. The more layers of laminate that you apply, the more porcelain-like the piece will become.

LAMP SHADE

1. If you are using a self adhesive lamp shade, peel the protective covering off and trace it onto the back side of the Ink Interlude paper, adding 1" all around for turning under. Otherwise, create your own pattern as described above. Cut pattern out.

2. Place Ink Interlude paper on lamp shade, right side out, and press the paper onto the shade, starting from the front and working to the back seams, being careful to roll the paper slowly onto the shade, pressing out air bubbles as you go. You will have a 1" extension at the top and bottom of the shade.

3. Make a number of small clips around the 1" extended paper at the top of the shade and fold to the inside, hot-gluing it in place.

4. Trim the bottom edge to ⅜" and turn under, again making clips where necessary, and hot-glue down.

RETRO FOUR-DRAWER CHEST

Any piece of furniture that has a number of drawers will work especially well with this collection of black-and-white geometric patterns. It has the stylish sophistication of a gentleman in a tuxedo. A pair of them flanking a bed would make great end tables, with just enough room for a reading light and a good book.

design tips:

- To top off your chest you could fold under and hot-glue the edges of the Pinstripe paper, then finish off the ends with some fabric fringe.
- For a bit more strength you could also iron on a fusible webbing to the back side of the paper.

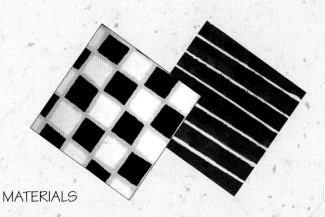

MATERIALS

. 1 sheet each Parisian Apartment Wallpapers: Black & White Checks, Black Tile, Pinstripe, Spots

. acrylic sealer

. black spray paint

. chest

. gluter

. paintbrush

. scissors

. white porcelain drawer pulls

INSTRUCTIONS

1. Clean chest and do any necessary repairs. Remove existing handles.

2. Cut each paper to fit the front of a drawer.

3. Paint chest black and let dry completely.

4. Coat the front of the drawers with gluter and adhere the papers to the drawer fronts.

5. Give the entire chest, including drawer fronts, several coats of sealer, allowing everything to dry between applications.

6. Attach the drawer pulls.

RETRO CLOCK

The clock was the finishing touch on our Retro Room. It would also look great in a man's office. We made ours on Plexiglas, but you could also use wood. Most glass places carry Plexiglas and will cut it to size for you.

MATERIALS

. 1 sheet each Parisian Apartment Wallpapers: Black & White Checks, Pinstripe, Spots

. 1 sheet Cloud Vanilla Handmade Paper (optional)

. 5' heavy gold cord

. 12" Plexiglas (or wood) circle with a ¼" hole drilled in center

. clockworks kit

. glue gun and glue sticks

. gluter

. ruler

. scissors

. small paintbrush

INSTRUCTIONS

1. For the clock background, cut a 15" x 7½" partial circle of the Checks paper, being certain to cut the paper so you leave a straight line of full squares approximately ½" from the top.

2. Cut a 15" x 6½" partial circle of the Pinstripe paper.

3. Cut a 2" x 15" strip of the Spots paper.

4. Using the small paintbrush, paint the entire surface of the Plexiglas clock base with gluter.

5. Gently position the Checks piece on the bottom half of the clock base, overlapping its outer edges.

6. Repeat with the Pinstripe piece on the top half of the clock base, leaving a narrow area between the two papers.

7. Paint the back side of the strip of Spots with the gluter and position it in the area between the other two papers, bringing the bottom edge of Spots down to the top of the row of checks on the lower half of the clock base.

8. Trim the overlapping paper to about ½" from the outer edges and glue in place.

9. Mark the center hole on your clock front and cut a small "X" at the hole area, trimming off the inner points.

10. Your clock kit will come with a face. We wanted a different look, so we photocopied the clock face onto a piece of Mandalay paper trimmed to 8½" x 11" to fit through the photocopy machine. Do not substitute a handmade paper that has a lot of fiber in it, as it may harm the machine.

11. Glue your clock face to the center of the clock base and again mark and cut an "X", trimming the points.

12. Hot-glue the heavy gold cord around the perimeter of the clock face, lightly unraveling the ends so that they can be woven together to form a smooth surface.

13. Repeat around the outer perimeter of the clock base.

14. Cut a 12" diameter circle of the Spots paper, paint with the gluter and cover the back of the clock base. When dry, cut the hole in the middle.

15. Following kit directions, insert clockworks and battery.

Reality Reminder:
Sit down before fact like a little child, and be prepared to give up every preconceived notion. Follow humbly wherever and to whatever abyss nature leads, or you shall learn nothing.

—T. H. Huxley

CHAPTER EIGHT

AFTERNOON LEMONADE SOCIAL

Picture ladies in long flowing skirts, cloche hats, and low-heeled strappy shoes, engaged in languid conversation with no cell phones or day books to interrupt the leisurely pace. That was our image for our Afternoon Lemonade Social. This is a delightful place to relax with a cool drink, an interesting read or an intriguing companion.

The secret to creating this mood is to use bright happy colors combined with natural, organic-looking materials. If you have a real "lemon" of a chair, you will definitely want to check out our Lemon Chair on page 98–99.

We REALLY wanted a lemon tree, but unfortunately they tend to be few and far between here in the Pacific Northwest, so we decided to make our own with a bit of tape, a load (actually a tree-load) of faux lemons, and a very accommodating weeping white birch.

We love the old café bentwood chairs; they have such a sidewalk bistro look to them and they are usually inexpensive and easy to locate at used restaurant supply houses. Our bistro table came together with three old windows that were topped with a wooden "round" available at most home building suppliers.

You may have noticed that we LOVE old windows and will look for any excuse to use them. Here we took three that were the same height and applied a wonderful handmade paper that has actual fern foliage embedded into the paper pulp: Coral Seas Botanikal Paper, "Sword Ferns" (see instructions for Wildflower Antique Window on page 80). We then hinged them together and placed a paper-covered table round on top (same technique as the one used to cover the Parisian Women Boudoir Chair on page 74). It is heavy enough that we didn't need to attach it to the windows.

LEMONADE SOCIAL TABLE

Anytime we have a chance to pick up old wooden windows, we grab 'em! There are so many wonderful things you can do with them. Here, we used a very simple technique to create a perfect little afternoon social table.

MATERIALS

. 3 old wooden windows, about 28" high

. 3 sheets sage soft-textured paper

. 3 sheets Sword Ferns Paper

. 6 double-swing hinges

. 6 egg whites

. acrylic sealer

. drill and screws

. gluter

. paintbrushes

. plywood circle, 32"–36" diameter

. ruler

. scissors

INSTRUCTIONS

1. Clean and repair windows, if necessary.

2. Cut Ferns paper to fit glass areas. Measure each window separately since the glass will often not be the same size.

3. Brush the glass with the egg whites and apply the paper, right side up. Gently work any air bubbles out to the side. Brush more egg white on top of the paper and let dry overnight. Trim excess paper along glass-pane edges.

4. Place the windows with glass side out in a triangle, then measure and mark the sides of the windows where you need to place the double hinges.

5. Screw the hinges on, making a triangular table base.

6. Distress the soft-textured paper and tear into workable 4"–6" pieces.

7. Dip the paper pieces one at a time into the gluter and apply to the plywood circle. Let dry over night.

8. Seal with 2–3 coats of acrylic sealer.

9. Place the tabletop on the base.

Reality Reminder:
HOW TO BE SUCCESSFUL:
· Work as though you don't need the money.
· Love like you've never been hurt.
· Dance as though no one is watching you.
—Unknown

LEMONADE SOCIAL PITCHER, GLASSES & PLACE MAT

Just looking at this pitcher and glasses makes you feel like you're in an old 1940s movie. You rather expect Katherine Hepburn and Cary Grant to come strolling out across the lawn, exchanging marvelously foolish banter. You can, of course, use any shape of pitcher and glasses, but we chose the old-style, classic belly shape because we really wanted this to have the flavor of an old-fashioned lemonade social.

The pitcher, glasses, and place mat all use the same papers. You can, of course, use any kind of paper; but you do want to choose ones that have a distinct pattern yet still have relatively simple lines.

The Place Mat on page 95 is a very quick and easy project, and the concept is one that you can use over and again with any theme you might have. If you are working with a paper with a strong color theme, you might also want to use two complementary colors for the actual mat, then cut out your patterns and glue them onto the mat's surface for a variation on this technique.

design tip:

- To make a quick-and-easy deckle edge anytime you need to, simply fold your paper, then run a damp sponge (even a fingertip will do) along the fold line. Allow a few seconds for the moisture to seep in, then gently, using both hands placed flat on the paper on either side of the fold, pull the two sides apart from each other.

MATERIALS

PITCHER & GLASSES

. 1 sheet cherry-patterned paper

. 1 sheet mauve soft-textured paper

. clear drinking glasses

. glass pitcher with wide center

. liquid laminate

. paintbrush

. scissors

PLACE MAT

. 1 sheet cherry-patterned paper

. 1 sheet mauve soft-textured paper

. liquid laminate

. paintbrush

INSTRUCTIONS

PITCHER & GLASSES

1. Cut cherries and leaves from the cherry-patterned paper.

2. Tear a 2"-wide strip of the mauve paper, long enough to girdle the belly of the pitcher.

3. Brush the back of the mauve paper strip with the laminate and wrap around the middle of the pitcher, pressing down all parts firmly.

4. Brush the backs of the cut-out cherries with laminate and place three bunches around the pitcher.

5. Do the same with several of the leaves, placing them at logical angles to the cherry bunches.

6. Carefully brush several coats of the laminate to the top of the papers, being careful not to brush it on the glass, and letting the laminate dry between coats. Using 4–6 coats of laminate will allow you to hand-wash the piece without damaging the paper design.

7. Follow the same procedure for the glasses, using one cherry bunch per glass.

PLACE MAT

1. Because we made our place mat to fit our rather small table, we used only half of each sheet of paper. If you are using less than the full sheet to make your place mat, fold both sheets to the desired size, with the mauve paper 4" longer and 4" wider than the cherry-patterned paper.

2. After folding the papers to size, tear along the folds to create a deckle edge. If the fold goes through some of the cherry pattern, cut the pattern area and let the pattern overlap onto the mauve border (this can add an interesting dimension to the finished place mat).

3. Brush the back side of the cherry-patterned paper with the laminate, and center it on the mauve paper, pressing any air bubbles out to the sides.

4. Brush several coats of laminate on the top of the place mat, allowing each coat to dry before applying the next one. Repeat with the back of the place mat.

LEMONADE SOCIAL CHAIR

We used an old bentwood chair that we found at a used restaurant supply store. Any old wooden chairs with removable seats would work equally well. The important thing is to be certain that they are sturdy and to make any structural repairs before you begin giving your chair a new identity.

MATERIALS

. 1 yard cherry-patterned fabric

. 2 sheets sage soft-textured paper

. chair with removable seat

. gluter

. scissors

. staple gun and staples

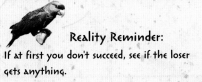

Reality Reminder:
If at first you don't succeed, see if the loser gets anything.

—Unknown

INSTRUCTIONS

1. Remove the seat from the chair. Clean and repair the chair if necessary.

2. Distress the paper and tear it into 4"–6" pieces.

3. Dip the paper pieces into the gluter and apply the papers to the frame of the chair, allowing the pieces to overlap. Cover completely and let dry overnight.

4. Place the seat on the fabric (as a template) and cut the fabric 4" larger than the seat. Be certain to center the seat on the part of the fabric pattern that you like.

5. Staple one spot on one side of the fabric to the underside of seat, then pull firmly across the top to opposite side and staple that point to underside. Repeat on the remaining two sides. Continue to staple around fabric edges by easing a little bit at a time, tucking and stapling as you go.

6. Reattach the seat to the chair.

LEMON CHAIR

We originally developed this fantasy chair for a French Country kitchen, which was done in the traditional blues, yellows, and golds of southern France. It is still one of our favorites, and as you might guess, we had as much fun photographing it as we did creating it. Our Wood Crated Lemons are very realistic; and since they are made of foam, they are very lightweight and easy to cut. However, most stores that carry a quality selection of silk flowers will also have faux fruits.

MATERIALS

. 1 package faux lemons

. 1 sheet Persimmon Quilt Paper

. 3 sheets Cobalt Quilt Paper

. chair with cushion, (preferably plastic or faux leather, not absorbent fabric)

. glue gun and glue sticks

. gluter

. hacksaw

INSTRUCTIONS

1. Remove the seat. Repair and clean the chair if necessary.
2. Tear the cobalt and persimmon papers into small workable pieces. Set the persimmon pieces aside.
3. Dip cobalt paper into the gluter and apply to the chair frame. Allow your pieces to overlap until you have covered the frame completely with paper. Let dry.
4. Dip the persimmon paper into the gluter and apply the paper to the seat cushion, allowing as much as 50% overlapping to add strength. Cover completely and let dry thoroughly.
5. Reattach seat to chair.
6. Cut the faux lemons lengthwise in half with saw.
7. Hot-glue the lemon halves to the back of chair in a row. Your design will depend on the style of the chair.

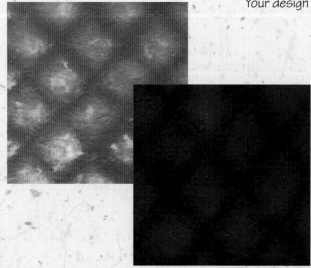

✂ design tips:

- We knew that our chair was going to be strictly decorative, so we did not bother to seal it. However, if you are planning to actually use yours, a couple of coats of an acrylic sealer will work beautifully, although it will slightly darken the paper colors.

- Rather than sitting on this chair, consider hanging it on a wall and using the seat as you would a shelf. In a kitchen, it might be a great place to keep a bowl of —what else?–lemons!

CHAPTER NINE

NOW & ZEN

She was slender, and although not tall, somehow had "presence." Long, straight black hair framed an oval face with black almond-shaped eyes. A sense of quiet calm surrounded her and infused the very air in her private room where a hint of sandalwood incense mingled with haunting yet soothing sounds of soft Oriental music. This was her special place, a room where everything reflected her inner thoughts and, no matter where her attention landed, her eyes rested on things of beauty.

We created a room similar to this a few years ago for The Christopher Lowell Show and it was called the "Room of Calm." If you have always longed for a quiet space that demands nothing more of you than to "be present," then many of our Now & Zen ideas should appeal to you. Add things that appeal to your senses, such as your favorite fragrances: if not incense, then perhaps a potpourri mix. Soft bamboo wind-chime sounds are extremely pleasant, yet not distracting. This is a room to listen to your own inner dialogue and maybe to record your observations and feelings. Most of all, it is somewhere to escape to when you need that "quiet place."

ORIENT EXPRESS PAPERS

Oriental design papers are one of our favorites to work with. We don't know what they say, but we do know that there is Korean, Chinese and Japanese scripts, all done in different handwriting, making them extremely individual and unique. One of the advantages of not being able to read the writing means that we just look at them as beautiful artwork.

Because the papers are fairly lightweight and porous, the inking process will bleed to the back side. Oftentimes, we have found this to be the more interesting side to work with, depending on the effect we were going for. The front (or right) side of the papers is clear and bold, and the back side is somewhat faded, with bits of design missing, etc., giving the entire paper a look of old parchment or ancient documents.

If you are a collector of bits of odd coins, scraps of metal and embellishments of all kinds, you'll find that these particular papers marry very well with your found objects.

NOW & ZEN DESK

The beauty and grace of Oriental writing figures makes them wonderful to use simply for their graphic appeal. I had worked out a design for the third volume of our Owner's Manual and we all liked it so much that we decided to use the same concept on a desk. Actually, this piece was an old sewing cabinet from the 1950s. We think its reincarnation is nothing less than FABULOUS!

When hunting for a piece to work on, look for items that have interesting features that you can accent with the papers: unusual handles, different-shaped drawers, etc.

MATERIALS

. 2 sheets soft-textured papers: papaya, antiqued plum

. 2 packages Burnt Persimmon Hana Hemp

. 6 sheets various Orient Express Papers

. acrylic paints: brown, olive, and mustard yellow

. acrylic sealer

. desk

. glue gun and glue sticks

. gluter

. newspaper

. paintbrush

. ruler

. scissors

. sponge

. tortoiseshell Japanese luck stone

INSTRUCTIONS

1. Work out a design for your desk, using different shapes of the papers to accent and draw attention to features on the piece you are working on.

2. Cut out your design pattern from the newspaper. Lay out on desk and make adjustments in the design before cutting the handmade papers.

3. Lightly distress the papers.

4. Dilute the paints, about 2:1 water and paint. Brush and sponge all the papers to dull down and "age" the papers. Allow the colors to blend and bleed. It is better to paint a little, let it dry, then add more paint. Let papers dry completely when finished.

5. Measure and cut out a piece of hemp long enough to go completely around your desk two times, plus an extra foot. Cut a second piece the same size.

6. Let the pieces of hemp soak for a few minutes in the watered-down paint to dull it down. The color will be different when dry, so let dry, then resoak as much as necessary to get the shade you want.

7. Cut out patterns in the Orient Express papers and the soft-textured papers, and lay out on desk to be sure it works and looks the way you anticipated. Make adjustments in design at this time.

8. Working in small areas at a time, brush gluter onto the desk surface and lay the papers down, gently brushing another layer of gluter on top. Work problem areas into place by carefully sponging them in.

9. Continue until the design is complete. Let dry and finish with the acrylic sealer.

10. Fold one piece of the dry hemp in half, slip the folded middle through the center hole in the stone, pull slightly through, then insert the two ends through the loop and pull tight, locking the hemp securely on one side of the stone (for old macramé adepts, this is a Lark's Head knot). Do the same thing with the remaining piece of hemp on the other side of the stone.

11. Position the stone in the top-front center of your desk and, keeping the hemp taut, bring the cords around to the back of the desk and tie off. Opening up the two stands of the hemp into a "V" as they move toward the edge of the desk will give the project a bit of extra flair.

 Reality Reminder:

When I am working on a problem I never think about beauty. I only think about how to solve the problem. But when I have finished, if the end result is not beautiful, I know it is wrong.
—Buckminster Fuller

✂ design tip:
• Wooden skewers are great tools to keep handy for working paper, glue, etc. into tiny corners and awkward spaces.

<u>NOW & ZEN DESK CHAIR</u>

This is a very classy look. We took an image and enlarged it about four times to get the look we wanted. Any image you like will work, but simple line drawings will be more effective than extremely detailed or busy designs.

This chair is one that was probably a kitchen reject from the 1950s. The simple two-rung back has an almost Oriental look to begin with.

MATERIALS

. 1 sheet Mocha Quilt Paper

. 2 sheets black soft-textured paper

. acrylic sealer

. chair with removable seat

. crane or other oriental image

. gluter

. iron-on fusible webbing

. iron-on interfacing

. paintbrush

. photocopier

. scissors

. staple gun and staples

INSTRUCTIONS

1. Remove the seat. Clean and repair chair if necessary.

2. Tear soft-textured paper into workable 2"–3" pieces.

3. Dip the paper pieces individually into the gluter and apply to the frame of the chair, covering the frame completely.

4. Let the chair dry overnight and seal with acrylic sealer.

5. Photocopy your image to enlarge it to the desired size. At this point you may want to take a black marker and darken or accent areas in the design.

6. Cut an 8½" x 11" piece of the mocha paper and run this piece, right side up, through the photocopier, copying your sized image onto the mocha paper.

7. Iron on the webbing to the back of the mocha paper image.

8. Deckle the edges of the mocha paper by tearing off all the straight edges.

9. Cut another piece of mocha paper, 24" x 24" and iron imaged mocha paper to the top (right side) of it.

10. Iron on the interfacing to the back side of the piece, making your seat cover.

11. Place this cover right side up on chair seat. Tuck papers to underside of seat and staple one point, pull taut and staple one point on opposite side. Repeat on the other two sides, then ease the corners down smooth and staple. Continue easing and stapling until cover is smooth and tight.

design tip:

• We tore around the desired image, then darkened the outline of the crane with a black permanent marker. As you enlarge your image, you may need to do more touch ups. As you can see, although the surrounding imagery is rather complex, the crane has simple lines, making it easy to distinguish.

WRAPPED ROCK PAPERWEIGHTS

A very quick-and-easy way to add a touch of Oriental flavor to a desk corner, etc., is to create these wrapped rocks. The only real trick here is to find smooth and relatively well-shaped rocks that are heavy enough to provide a paperweight function, but not so heavy that they are awkward.

✂ design tips:

- We used rocks that were approximately 4"–5" long. An interesting variation would be to use smaller stones, wrapped in various papers, to fill a glass bowl or compote.
- We used some of the same papers to cover alternating panels on a glass compote, then filled the compote with our Zen Spheres.
- You could easily create your own spheres by covering an assortment of Styrofoam balls with the papers of your choice.

INSTRUCTIONS

1. Wash rocks and let dry.
2. Distress papers and tear into small workable pieces.
3. Dip paper into the gluter and apply to the stone, using different papers on the same stone to give it a random collage look. Let dry completely.
4. Apply a minimum of three coats of acrylic sealer. Let dry between coats.

MATERIALS

. 2–3 softball-sized river rocks
. 3 sheets various Orient Express Papers
. acrylic sealer
. gluter
. paintbrush

ORIENTAL HOUSE BANNER

We have always been attracted to the banners and signs that decorate the outsides of Japanese shops. Although our version in no way compares to the authentic "noren" of Japanese tradition, it was still this beautiful form of early advertising and privacy that inspired us to create a hanging banner of our own.

MATERIALS

. 1 sheet antiqued plum soft-textured paper

. 1 sheet mocha soft-textured paper

. 1 sheet mustard yellow handmade paper

. 1 sheet Orient Express Paper

. dowel, ¼" x 36"

. glue gun and glue sticks

. paintbrush

. premixed water-based wallpaper paste

. scissors

INSTRUCTIONS

1. Fold down 1½" along the 25" side of the plum paper to the back side of the paper and hot-glue along the underside edge, forming a casing for the dowel.

2. Deckle the edges of the mocha paper, making it approximately 24" x 31½". Using the wallpaper paste, adhere this to the top of the plum paper. Let dry.

3. Deckle the edges of the mustard paper to make a sheet approximately 23" x 30" and paste this to the top of the mocha paper. Let dry.

4. Cut the Orient Express paper 22" x 29½" and paste it to the top of the other papers. Let dry.

5. Insert the dowel through the casing and hang.

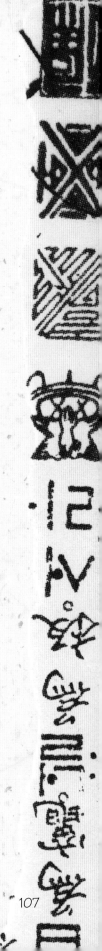

ORIENTAL WALL PANELS: COLLAGE & MONTAGE

I have to tell you, once I got started making these wall panels there was no stopping me—the possibilities were just SO enticing! Because we wanted ours to be movable, we worked on the insulation panels that can be purchased at any building supply store. If you want something a bit more permanent, you could, of course, use the same technique directly onto your walls. Just be certain to apply a strippable wallpaper liner first so you can remove it later if desired.

The brown kraft paper will be necessary if, like us, you can only find insulation panels in pink (which will show through if not covered). If your panels are white, the kraft paper is probably not needed.

The Montage panel is essentially done in the same manner as the Collage one, except that we only worked with one of the Orient Express papers, then added a montage of some antique postcard images, some Japanese Luck Stones and bits and pieces of other papers, including our original mock-ups for our catalogue.

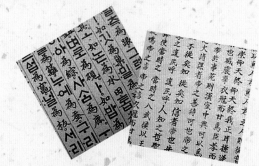

MATERIALS

COLLAGE

. 1 sheet each of various Orient Express Collection Papers

. 18' brown kraft paper (if necessary)

. 5 sheets of one Orient Express Paper

. insulation foam panels, 2' x 2" x 8'

. premixed water-based wallpaper paste

. sponge brushes

MONTAGE

. 1 each various Japanese Luck stones

. 5 sheets of one Orient Express Paper. 18' brown kraft paper (if necessary)

. insulation panels, 2' x 2" x 8'

. glue gun and glue sticks

. premixed, water based wallpaper paste

. sponge brushes

. various images

INSTRUCTIONS

COLLAGE

1. Apply the wallpaper paste to the panel and adhere the brown kraft paper to the front of the panel.

2. Turn panel over and do the same to the back, finishing edges and ends off by tucking and pasting them down flat, covering all of the panel's surface.

3. Paste the five same-patterned Orient Express papers right side down, giving the piece an aged appearance. Cover the front and sides completely and let dry.

4. Cut the various Oriental papers into different sizes and paste them onto the covered panel.

5. Let dry overnight.

MONTAGE

1. Follow Steps 1–3 above for Collage, using the Orient Express papers.

2. Apply paste to the back of the images and paste into a gallery on the panel.

3. Hot-glue the stones to the panels. You may want to run twines, trims, other pieces of handmade paper, etc., on the surface, creating your own design.

ORIENTE EXPRESS PAPERS

JAPANESE LUCK STONES

CHINESE FANTAN
WALL PLAQUE

This was a wonderful old image depicting a group of Chinese men engaged in a game of Fantan, probably around 1905 or so. The image was so interesting that we decided to use it as the basis for a wall plaque, which we then decided to use on our desk instead. Of course, you could use any image that catches your fancy, but the coloration on the old sepia-toned cards looks really wonderful. If you want an aged-parchment look, use the reverse side of the paper. The right side will give you a crisper, cleaner look. The Bark Ribbon is real tree bark that has been laminated to a paper background, then finished on the edges with a jute lashing.

We used a piece of the same type of insulation board that we discussed when making the Oriental Wall Panels on pages 108–109. It is light, inexpensive, and SO easy to work with.

MATERIALS

. 1 Bark and Twine Ribbon

. 1 sheet Orient Express Paper

. 1 vintage image

. acrylic sealer

. brown kraft paper (optional)

. glue gun and glue sticks

. gluter

. insulation foam board, 8" x 2" x 12"

. Japanese luck stones: 1 bone, 2 charcoal

. premixed water-based wallpaper paste

. sponge brush

INSTRUCTIONS

1. Apply wallpaper paste liberally to the board. If your board is colored, you must first cover the entire piece with brown kraft paper.

2. Depending on the effect you want, use either the right or wrong side of the Orient Express paper and paste it down over the board (or kraft paper). Let dry overnight.

3. Center and paste down the image.

4. Hot-glue stones to the right-hand side of the image, placing the bone in the middle. The image we were working with had a perfect place on the right side to add the stones. If your image does not, place it so that you leave approximately a 3" border on the side for the stones.

5. Brush on acrylic sealer.

6. Hot-glue the ribbon around all sides of the plaque.

MEDITATION JOURNAL

The room is quiet, a hint of jasmine teases the air, a cup of soothing Oolong tea sits nearby, and this time belongs to you alone—a time to reflect and perhaps commit a few thoughts to your journal.

MATERIALS

. 1 sheet bamboo ocher paper

. 2 chopsticks

. 10 bamboo paperclips

. black ink

. glue gun and glue sticks

. Oriental script stencil

. palm fiber

. premixed water-based wallpaper paste

. saddle-stitched journal

. tiny beach glass disk

INSTRUCTIONS

1. Cut a piece of palm fiber to fit the front of the journal.

2. Apply the wallpaper paste to the back of the fiber, slip three of the paperclips onto the fiber and paste it down firmly on the front of the journal. Depending on the shape of the fiber piece, you may want to angle it to create more visual interest.

3. Tear a piece of the paper to fit the upper-right corner of the journal.

4. Stencil the Oriental script onto this piece of paper and distress it when ink is dry.

5. Paste this to the upper-right corner of the journal.

6. Hot-glue the chopsticks to top of the journal at the edge of the spine.

7. Center and hot-glue the glass disk to the center left side, next to the chopsticks.

111

CHAPTER TEN

BEACH PARTY

"Come to a beach party," the invitation read, "we will have a fish barbecue and clam bake, crabs and canapés, lobsters and lively music, good conversation and warm evening breezes. All that will be missing is the ocean. Bring your appetite and imagination."

We had our "beach party, sans beach" next to a creek in our Bamboo Teahouse. Sounds of water gurgling over rocks substituted for the crash of waves, green grass tickled our toes instead of sand, and tall cottonwoods stood in for dune grass and seaweed.

Creating a seashore mood was easy with strings of FABULOUS faux fish hung everywhere. A really big one (that didn't get away) had the evening's menu glued to his side and one of those famous "flying fish" you hear about miscalculated and ended up doing a deep dive into a basket of daisies.

We carried out our theme with bamboo and coconut serving pieces, then teamed these up with inexpensive glass plates (and plastic goblets) turned into festive beachy dinnerware. When evening arrived and the party moved indoors, froths of seashell-studded fabric provided a suitable backdrop for some very "fishy" lights stacked on some bamboo tables.

Lack of a nearby ocean should never be a deterrent for a good beach party. With a scrap of fishnet, a few shells, some creatively utilized fish, appropriate lighting, a healthy dose of imagination, and a bit of poetic license, you are on your way!

RIGHT: The frothy fabric in the background is shell fabric, which is available as both fabric (for your own projects) and as curtains, which can then be used as a background or space dividers.

When the party moves indoors, you will need some illumination, and we have created just the thing. You can easily make one (or all three) of our Beach Party Lamps. You will notice that we have used three different sizes and shapes of shades; but all are the self-adhesive variety, making the job VERY easy. If you can't find this item in a size that works, or if you happen to have a fabulous old shade that needs a new life, you can easily make a pattern. Lay the shade on its side on your paper, and while rolling the shade, mark the path with a pencil about 1" from the shade's bottom edge. Then reverse the roll and do the same thing for the top edge.

One idea just naturally leads to another, and you will find that as you start thinking along these lines, your imagination just keeps coming up with more "beachy" ideas. What about a seaweed lamp, or maybe one studded with driftwood bits or found agates, or, or, or...

BEACH PARTY TABLETOP

Our tabletop really sets the mood for our beach party theme. You could use the same techniques and change the atmosphere simply by using other colors and different papers when making your dinner plates and goblets.

✂ design tips:

• Be sure to pick out papers that are bright and contrast dramatically with each other for your two different plates.

• If you can't find anything with a fish design, you can easily stencil or freehand your fish, shells, etc., on a paper of your choice.

MATERIALS

LINENS

. 1 yard seashell-patterned cotton fabric

. 1 yard soft burlap cloth

PLATES

. 2 sheets Rainbow Fish Hand-painted Paper

. 2 sheets Sunrise Batik Paper

. 4 glass dessert-sized plates

. 4 glass dinner-sized plates

GOBLETS

. 2 sheets Rainbow Fish Hand-painted Paper

. 4 goblets, (we bought plastic)

FISH CENTERPIECE WITH MENU

. 1 large faux fish

. 1 sheet lightweight handmade paper

. 20' Natural Abaca Twine

. assorted small faux fish

GENERAL MATERIALS

. large sponge

. liquid laminate

. paintbrush

INSTRUCTIONS

LINENS

1. To make your tablecloth, cut the burlap into a 36" square and fringe all sides. Select a burlap with a medium-loose weave, making it ideal for fringing.

2. Tear four 2" x 18" strips of the cotton for tying the coconut flatware together at each place setting.

PLATES

1. Place a dessert plate upside down on Rainbow paper, centering your design over one of fish, and tracing around the plate about ¼" beyond the edge. Cut out four of these circles.

2. Spread a light coat of the laminate on the under side of dessert plates. Make certain edges are covered completely.

3. Place each circle of paper on the bottom of the plates (right side down to show through the plate) and press into place, working all air bubbles out from the middle to the edges with a large damp sponge.

4. Brush 3–5 generous layers of laminate over the paper, allowing it to dry between applications. The plates are now hand-washable.

5. Apply the Sunrise papers to the dinner plates, using the same process.

GOBLETS

1. Cut circle to fit the bottom of the goblets, centering circle on the spiral design on the paper. Apply the circle to the bottom of a goblet using the same technique as for the plates, finishing with the 3–5 coats of liquid laminate.

design tip:

- We hung our "catch" from the center of the ceiling in our Bamboo Teahouse. Depending on where your beach party happens, you could utilize a light fixture, open beams, or a ceiling hook. If nothing overhead is an option, try filling a large bucket with beach sand, then anchor a couple of slender bamboo in the sand and hang your "catch" off these makeshift fishing poles.

FISH CENTERPIECE WITH MENU

1. Write or print your menu on handmade paper and center it so that it is about the width of the fish's side. We typed ours on a computer, using a scrawl font, then printed it out and photocopied it onto the handmade paper. We then tore the menu out so that it would have a jagged edge.

2. Brush a light coat of the laminate onto the side of the fish and gently place the menu on the fish's side. Let dry, then seal the menu with another coat of laminate.

3. Tie all the faux fish individually by their tails with different lengths of twine. Then tie all the strands together at the top and hang over the table.

FISH NAPKIN
WEIGHT

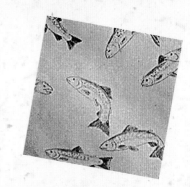

A few years ago, Art and I were traveling in the hills of Tuscany and ended up at a delightful inn, set picturesquely on the edge of the family's ancient (yet still producing) olive groves. Before dinner was served, everyone sat out on the piazza, sipping an assortment of the local wines and munching on—what else?—olives. The evening was warm but breezy; and to keep the paper napkins from scattering into the groves, a number of medium-sized field stones had been hand-painted with olive images and were used to weight down anything that could blow away.

We were enchanted with this idea, so simple yet practical. Since we get some fairly lively breezes by our creek, too, we decided to do a "fishy" version of the napkin weights for our Beach Party.

INSTRUCTIONS

1. Distress the paper and tear off all straight edges.

2. Tear the paper into workable 3"–4" pieces. Make sure that you have a number of full fish images.

3. Dip the paper pieces into the gluter and smooth them onto the stone. Allow some of the pieces to wrinkle and work wrinkles down flat on the stone to create texture.

4. Continue placing the paper pieces on the stone, overlapping the papers until it is completely covered, then top the stone with a few of the more complete images.

5. Let dry completely.

6. Water down the acrylic paint and sponge it onto the dry stone. You may want to let it dry between applications as the color intensity will change as it dries.

7. Continue adding the diluted paint until all the cracks and crevices formed by the wrinkles are defined.

8. Let dry, then seal.

MATERIALS

. 1 sheet Fish Project Paper

. acrylic paint: slate or charcoal

. acrylic sealer

. gluter

. smooth stone, 4"–5"

RAFFIA & ROCK SNAIL LAMP SHADE

With its fringed skirt, this would be a great lamp for a Hawaiian Luau party! Although this looks a bit complicated, it is actually a very easy project, but the raffia fringe is a bit time consuming. It's an ideal evening project to settle in with while watching a good movie.

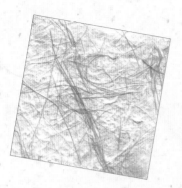

MATERIALS

. 1 sheet Fall Grass Textured Fibre Paper

. 3 hanks natural raffia

. 100 rock snail shells

. abaca braid, 14" x 20'

. glue gun and glue sticks

. large craft (doll making) needle

. liquid laminate

. scissors

. small self-adhesive lamp shade

 design tip:
• We liquid-laminated the same Textured Fibre Handmade Paper to the base of this lamp, using small torn pieces of the paper. When finished, it had a wonderful nubby, almost seaweed look to it.

INSTRUCTIONS

1. Follow Steps 1–4 for the Baby Fish & Fishnet Lamp Shade on page 121.

2. Cut a piece of braid 6"–8" longer than the circumference of the bottom edge of lamp shade.

3. Fold raffia in half one strand at a time, and loop it over the abaca braid, pulling raffia ends through the loop (a Lark's Head knot for you macramé fans).

4. Tighten knot down and continue until the braid is covered, leaving 3"–4" at each end uncovered.

5. Divide the knots into groups of 20 and trim into a point (long in the middle and getting shorter approaching knot #1 and knot #20). This won't be exact, but that is part of its charm, so don't get too picky here.

6. Hot-glue the shells to the ends of the raffia strands: one shell per strand for a full fringe, or every other one if you want a lighter look.

7. Hot-glue fringe to bottom edge of lamp shade, then hot-glue a braid just above fringe to finish the edges.

8. Hot-glue another piece of braid to top of shade with shells hot-glued every 1½".

BABY FISH & FISHNET LAMP SHADE

Little tropical fish swim along the rim of this handmade-paper lamp shade, overlaid with a piece of jute fishnet. This paper has a lightly crinkled texture with specks of real shell sprinkled on the surface, giving it the appearance of sun-kissed water.

We nestled our Baby Fish & Fishnet Lamp into a corner and hung a big string of faux fish next to it to carry out our fishy theme. All our faux fish, including the "Baby" ones, are made of a foam resin with real cornhusk for their tails and fins (so real only your nose knows for sure).

MATERIALS

. 1 sheet Guava Shell Paper

. assorted faux baby fish

. doubleknot fishnet

. glue gun and glue sticks

. glue stick

. pencil

. scissors

. self-adhesive lamp shade,
  4" x 11" x 7"

INSTRUCTIONS

1. Peel off protective paper from lamp shade, and using as a pattern, trace and cut shape from paper, cutting 1" larger than the template.

2. Place the cut-out paper right side out, onto the sticky surface of the shade and hand-press into place, starting at the front and working to the back seam. Leave a 1" extension at the top and the bottom of shade.

3. Trim bottom edge to ⅜", clip, turn under, and glue down.

4. Glue back seam with glue stick. Clip top edge about every ½". Glue top and bottom edges to inside of shade, rolling paper snuggly over the wire edge.

5. Cut a 12" x 36" piece of fishnet.

6. Starting at the back of lamp shade, hot-glue the net into place by gluing the knots to the shade. Trim ends of net to 1" at the edge, and hot-glue to inside of lamp shade.

7. At rim of shade, hot-glue baby fish to the lamp shade, alternating the colors.

design tips:

• In a darkened room the baby fish and the net become silhouetted with a soft, ocean green glow coming through the shade.

• For our lamp base, we used Lilac Quilt Paper, torn into small pieces and adhered with the liquid laminate. This paper looks almost like marble when it is applied this way.

FISH LAMP

It is a never ending source of amazement to us: all the things you can do with fish! Of course fresh ones spoil rather quickly, but our faux fish look so real that we often have people come up and try to discreetly give them a sniff.

MATERIALS

. 2 Rainbow Faux Fish

. 2 sheets Ocean Batik Paper

. 3 medium Silverside Faux Fish

. glue gun and glue sticks

. glue stick

. lamp base

. liquid laminate

. paintbrush

. scissors

. self-adhesive lamp shade, 4" x 16" x 9"

INSTRUCTIONS

1. The paper shade protector is your pattern. Peel from shade and trace it on back side of the paper, adding 1" all around. Cut out.

2. Place the paper cutout right side out onto the sticky surface of the shade and hand-press into place, starting at the front and working to the back seam. Leave a 1" extension at the top and the bottom of shade.

3. Using the glue-stick, adhere the back seam together.

4. Make small clips at the top edge of the paper and fold to inside, hot-gluing it in place.

5. Trim bottom edge to ⅜", clip, turn under, and glue down.

6. Hot-glue Silverside fish and then Rainbow fish evenly around the lamp shade, allowing the fish to "fringe" over the edge by a couple of inches. Set aside.

7. Tear the second sheet of paper into small workable pieces.

8. Brush the lamp base with the laminate. Place a paper piece on the laminate and brush the paper on. Continue adding paper pieces and laminate, lapping the papers over each other, until completely covered. Finish with another 1–2 coats of the laminate and let dry.

ABOVE: Silverside Fish.
RIGHT: Rainbow Fish.

122

design tips:

• We decided to cover this lamp base with another sheet of the Ocean Batik Paper, torn
  into small pieces and applied to the lamp base with the liquid laminate. The paper will
  have the same colors, but darker than they appear in the shade.

• You can paint your lamp base to pick up the color in your shade (or your fish).

Reality Reminder:
Life is not about finding yourself.
Life is about creating yourself.
—George Bernard Shaw

ABOVE: "Stay Cricket, stay, sit, sit Cricket, sit...stay, good dog, GOOD dog!"

ABOUT THE AUTHOR

Sandi Reinke is the senior designer and co-owner with her husband Art, of **loose ends**, an innovative company that has never really figured out if they are a design, a craft, or a home accessory company. The playful vision of the owners and unusual perspective of the company has enabled loose ends projects and products to appear regularly in such magazines as Women's Day, Romantic Homes, Better Homes & Gardens, Sunset, Country Living, Country Home, etc.

Sandi is a frequent guest on a number of "how-to" television shows, including The Carol Duvall Show, Decorating with Style, The Christopher Lowell Show, and others. Sandi and Art's passion for handmade items of all kinds, especially paper, takes the two of them to remote areas to work with the local village artists. When not traveling to "You're going WHERE?" they live with their blind watchdog Cricket and their fat cat Jiminey in Salem, Oregon.

THANKS

loose ends is a group effort, and without the support of everyone here, this book could not have come together as it did.

…Many thanks to the staff, especially Sarah, who was able to pick up my thread of thought and weave it into the tapestry that was in my head without much help from me.

…To Jason, **loose ends**' operations manager, who kept reminding me when the book drafts were due.

…To Jo, president of Chapelle, who simply was sure that I could get this book together with no problem at all, and proceeded with that assumption.

…To Diane, who did all the photography and is truly an artist with her camera. She quickly saw where we were going and not only joined in, but added her own quirky vision to the projects.

…To Cricket, our Yorkie, who although bored to tears with most of our activities during the hectic shooting days, still agreed to grace us with a few poses.

…To Roscoe, (posthumously) our parrot who shared our lives (riding to and from work everyday on a trash can) for almost 30 years, sharing his unique observations on life in his Reality Reminders.

…To my parents, Herb and Dee Williams, who gave me the genetic programming to love STUFF!

…And the most special thanks to Art, my husband and partner in both business and life, without whose nudging (sometimes pushing) this book would never have gotten past the idea stage.